Language Today

A SURVEY OF CURRENT LINGUISTIC THOUGHT

LANGUAGE
TODAY *A Survey*
of Current Linguistic Thought

MARIO PEI

Editor and Chief Contributor

OTHER CONTRIBUTORS

William F. Marquardt

Katharine Le Mée

Don L. F. Nilsen

FUNK & WAGNALLS

NEW YORK

Language Today
A Survey of Current Linguistic Thought

Library of Congress Catalog No. 67-26447

The quotation from "Dear Abby" on p. 131 is reprinted by permission of Abigail Van Buren, Internationally Syndicated Columnist.

Illustrations by George Bakacs

Contents

Foreword

It is the purpose of this book to present in simplified form and in layman's language a few of the more important language problems facing today's speakers of English.

Only a few could be presented, because language is a thing of many facets, and lends itself to a multiplicity of treatments. Paramount in the interest of the cultured layman are such things as the problem of usage; the question of sounds and spelling; that entrancing field known to the linguists as paralinguistics (all the meaning-carrying devices that are not part of the actual speech sounds); the problem of meaning itself; the views of grammar that have prevailed throughout history.

The question of usage has been presented from two different angles that I would describe as complementary rather than conflicting, by two writers whose views diverge in spots, one being more traditional and conservative, the other more liberal and permissive. But what seemed of even greater importance than a mere restatement of two positions that have often been stated was an analysis of the points of view held by people who are not linguists, and who must nevertheless use the language—the sort of thing they particularly object to in modern treatments of usage, their reaction to such novel tools of usage as the new *Webster's Third New International*

Dictionary. The handling Professor Marquardt and I have given the subject is admittedly far from exhaustive; still less is it meant to settle anything. But we hope that it will serve to clarify the issues and bring them into sharper focus.

The question of English sounds and English spelling, fraught with overtones of spelling reform and what can be done to bring the spoken and the written language into closer alignment, is one that has troubled English speakers from the days of Mulcaster to the recent pronouncements of G. B. Shaw. A review of this thorny issue is never amiss, particularly if accompanied by some sort of historical survey.

Linguists and nonlinguists alike are fascinated by those devices, semilinguistic, gestural, postural, symbolical, which serve to add meaning to the bare sounds that issue from a speaker's lips, or to bypass those sounds altogether, and indicate, deliberately or accidentally, the attitudes and emotional states of the individual who is trying to communicate. Here we have such topics as Kinesics, the study of gesture and posture in relation to the meaning the individual is trying to convey, or even to conceal; the semantic overtones that are supplied by pitch, rapidity of speech, loudness, intonation, even by such things as coughs and giggles. A great deal of scientific work has been done lately in this once almost neglected area. Mrs. Le Mée, a specialist in the field, brings to the reader the latest findings of her fellow researchers in the domain of paralinguistics.

Semantics is what supplies language with its *raison d'être.* The transfer of meaning from one human mind to another is basic in human communication and collaboration. But semantics has numerous subdivisions. There is the historical study of how words and expressions change their meaning, sometimes drastically. There is the area of diplomatic language, fraught with cautious understatement designed not to upset international applecarts in various states of unstable equilibrium. There is the language of propaganda, political, governmental, commercial, religious, and of many other kinds, whereby words are deliberately wrenched out of their original meaning or environment, endowed with varying degrees of guilt by association, made to represent what they did not formerly convey. There are the special jargons of specific occupations, and even of the sexes and age groups, whereby a word that means one thing to the physician will mean something altogether different to the engineer, a husband and wife will be talking at cross-purposes, and a teen-ager will seem not to recognize the vocabulary of his elders, while at the same time he creates a new vocabulary that is quite unintelligible to them. There is the entrancing field of cultural misunderstanding, wherein two subcultures of the same broad group fail utterly to grasp each other's meaning.

Finally, there is the official codification of language known as grammar, which in the course of centuries has shifted back and forth from one set of terms and definitions to another, and often back again. Here another specialist, Professor Nilsen, provides the reader with the background necessary to an understanding of the modern concept of grammar and its proper relation with the older grammatical tradition, as well as with the transitional forms that have held sway over the past four decades.

Language Today is accordingly designed to be a general summation of those phases of language which are of most direct concern to the person who is not a language specialist. My associates and I present it in a spirit of humility for what concerns its content, of confident expectation for what regards its immediate purpose of clarification and discussion.

In closing, I should like to express my appreciation to Sidney Landau, editor in chief of Funk & Wagnalls' dictionaries, for his valuable suggestions and advice during the editing of this book.

MARIO PEI
May 1967

Chapter 1

Is Language Abused? Two Points of View

MARIO PEI

Rightly or wrongly, a strong impression exists in many quarters that the English language is currently being mishandled; worse yet, abused.

How can a language be abused? Obviously, abuse can occur only concomitantly with use. Languages have been used by their speakers since the beginning of language. How those speakers use the language is just as obviously their own business. If linguists of different persuasions are correct in restricting the uses of language to communication and self-expression, then any use of language must serve either or both of those purposes. If communication between speakers of the same language is attained (that is, if there is accurate transfer of meaning from one mind to another through the instrumentality of language, spoken or written), or if the individual using language in either of its two main forms succeeds in expressing his inmost feelings to his own satisfaction, whether anyone else understands him or not, then the basic functions of language are served. When language is used to fulfill one of its functions, it cannot by definition be abused.

1

This is the stand taken by most descriptive linguists, that is, linguists who attempt to describe the linguistic structures that characterize specific languages and language in general. It is all right as far as it goes. But those who claim language is being abused oppose this attitude on two grounds: (1) there are uses of language, for either communication or self-expression, that are esthetically displeasing, logically inaccurate, or grammatically incorrect; (2) there are uses of language which lend themselves to misunderstanding and confusion. These two uses constitute a misuse and an abuse of language.

The first of these charges involves what the descriptive linguists call value judgments. A value judgment is subjective. It represents an individual's own personal reaction to what another individual does or says, or to a general situation. Being subjective and personal, a value judgment has no true objective or scientific value. One person's reaction may differ widely from another's. In a democratic, equalitarian society, one person is as good as another, and his judgment or reaction has equal value with anyone else's.

This is the sort of argument that can go on forever without a conclusion being reached. Those who claim that certain uses of language constitute abuse bring into play arguments of preparation, education, expertise, skill in using the language. They claim that by reason of all these factors some people are better qualified to handle language than others; that their usage should therefore prevail over that of the others; that they should be empowered to set themselves up as authorities as to what is "good" and "bad" or "correct" and "incorrect" in the matter of language; and that those less skilled and qualified should accept and follow their lead. Analogies are adduced aplenty. In warfare, privates, less qualified in tactics and strategy, follow the lead of their commanding officers, who know more. In medicine, a physician, endowed with years of specialized training, tells his unendowed patient what to do, and is obeyed. In construction, work crews follow the directions of the engineers. And so on.

To these arguments the opponents reply that language is in a different category from mathematics, physics, medicine, or military science; that language is a common tool for its users, and the users should be left free to reshape the tool in accordance with their own needs and convenience; that so long as the basic purposes of transfer of meaning and self-expression are served, the form matters little. They go on to point out that in the past, language has always been reshaped by its users, despite all the objections of the purists (were this not so, English speakers would today still be speaking Anglo-Saxon, and Romance speakers Latin).

All in all, the esthetic and historical field, while it lends itself beautifully to extended and even highly interesting discussion, does not seem to lead to ultimate conclusions. A better case, perhaps, can be made for the other claim: that some uses of language can be described as abuses because they engender confusion and misunderstanding.

Take, for example, the widespread current confusion of two words, *uninterested* and *disinterested*. The first means, traditionally, apathetic, and may be paraphrased by the expression "I don't care; it makes no difference to me." The second, traditionally, means impartial, open-minded, having no personal ax to grind, having nothing to gain or lose. But one can be disinterested and still be highly interested. If I am called upon to act as a juror in a case at law, I should by all means be disinterested, under penalty of being disqualified; I should not at all be uninterested; on the contrary, I should listen attentively as the evidence is presented, so that my final decision may serve the cause of justice. If a judge or arbiter is described as being disinterested, he is being paid a high compliment; if he is described as being uninterested, the description verges on insult; at the very least, he is being inefficient in his work.

*   *   *

One of the chief charges leveled against *Webster's Third New International Dictionary*, constructed by descriptive linguists and embodying the doctrine of unrestricted usage, is that it obliterates all, or most, of the value judgments of the past, reflected in earlier dictionaries by such labels as "slang," "vulgarism," "colloquialism," widely applied to certain words, and designed to act as guidelines to the users of what constitutes the "best" or "approved" or "cultivated" usage. The compilers of *Webster's Third* accept without flinching such uses as *like a cigarette should, He ain't here,* or *Who did you see?* which earlier dictionaries would have condemned as vulgarisms or colloquialisms on the ground that, however widespread, they do not reflect the norm of more educated speakers. It will be observed that these so-called vulgarisms leave the message perfectly clear. The same applies to such forms as *OK* and *to contact,* to such constructions as *It's me, between you and I, I laid on the bed for an hour.* The use of such "vulgarisms" may reflect upon their user to the extent of revealing to his hearer that he is either not as well educated as he might be or is a linguistic nonconformist. This may damage the speaker in his social or professional contacts. It does no real harm to the language, whose function is to be either meaningful or self-expressive. The critics, however, point out that the user of a dictionary is entitled to guidelines as to what is the most socially acceptable usage, and then be left free to choose for himself.

The second and more valid objection to *Webster's Third* is its obliteration of useful distinctions of meaning on the ground that those distinctions were being obliterated by the speakers themselves. Here its critics stood on firmer ground, as indicated by the widespread, often literary confusion of *uninterested* with *disinterested.*

But dictionary definitions are far from being the only area in which language is being abused, according to some critics. There is the whole world of language distortions stemming from the commercialistic jargon of advertising, the gobbledygook of government agencies, and the coinages of scholarly disciplines, including education, science, and pseudoscience. Taboo words and the euphemisms used to replace them, daring coinages by individuals, the press, and other communications media, the "weasel words" of national and international politics—all constitute additional areas of actual and potential abuse. The feeling of disquiet that prevails on the linguistic front is paralleled only by the similar feeling that pervades our political and international scene, where many think the world is going to pot, while just as many look forward to a bright new dawn of peace, brotherhood, and good feeling.

It may be well before we try to make pronouncements to glance at a cross section of opinion, view some of the specific objections of those who object to what is going on, and see what valid defense, if any, is made by those who are satisfied with the way things are.

In a *Saturday Review* article of May 14, 1966, entitled "Like *Your* Cigarette Should," editor Richard L. Tobin came to this melancholy conclusion: "There's no question that *like* for *as, as if,* and *as though* is a vulgarism, an usurper, but that's what usage is." He had previously quoted extensively from Bergen Evans, generally recognized as the foremost Apostle of Usage. His attitude of resigned condemnation, however, did not sit too well with many of his readers, as evidenced by entire columns of comments in a later issue. One writer, highly sarcastic, starts: "Like us permissivists say"; he goes on to feature "returning back," "in regards to," "consensus of opinion," "equally as good," "neither of them are no good," "who they can turn to," "all kinds of preventatives"; and he concludes: "Have faith in we permissivists, who try to be scientifically uninterested; the people have got to express themselves democratic-like!" Another writer tersely states: "Winston tastes bad, like a cigarette ad." Then there is a rash of mixed objections: "ask anyone what they think," "without me being there," even

Billy Graham's "and may the Lord bless you real good"! A few criticisms bear on matters of pronunciation of individual words, such as desPICable and stummick; even PULLitzer, which, after all, represents the original German pronunciation better than the PEW-litzer favored by most speakers. *Go a step further* and *further down the road* also come in for a drubbing, though the distinction between *further* and *farther* became dim in the dim past.

An even more literate series of objections to assorted vulgarisms transpires (here the British purists would object) from a list of comments submitted to the editorial board of an important publishing house by their dictionary consultants. Here, as one might expect, it is the confusing, ambivalent usages that draw the most withering barrage. (In connection with *bimonthly* used in the sense of twice a month as well as that of every two months one of the *Saturday Review* critics had remarked: "It should mean every two months; but some honest citizens think it means twice a month, so Gove [Philip B. Gove, editor in chief of *Webster's Third New International Dictionary*] says it sometimes means that.") In the consultants' poll, James Newman remarks: "The fact that the language is idiotic is no reason for us to be." Robert Saudek, rejecting the "twice a month" interpretation, says: "No; no more than I would allow double to mean half." Jacques Barzun adds: "In numerical sense, *no* concession to misconception can be made without endless misunderstanding and confusion." And Barbara Tuchman inquires: "How can it mean both? Black cannot also mean white!"

Barbara Tuchman's comment on *OK, Okay, Okeh* is: "The only excuse for these is laziness." Gilbert Highet, with his fine historical sense, has this to say about the use of *outside of* for *outside*: "Multiplication of prepositions is always a sign of decay in a language." For *to author,* his comment is: "Disgusting—like *gifted* him" (one might perhaps add *to father,* as in "He fathered her child," to the collection, and turn it into an unholy trinity). This type of functional change is satirized by Barzun in connection with "The Philharmonic will première two works" in these words: "And derrière them at the same time?" K. A. Porter calls *busing* "ghastly," while Walter Kerr, preferring the alternative spelling *bussing*, says: "How about a kiss?" Red Smith, confronted with "He invited Henry and myself," comments: "*Myself* is the refuge of idiots taught early that *me* is a dirty word." *Media* used as a singular, with a plural *medias*, gets this from Herbert Bruckner: "Used only by modern sociologists, who never had first-year Latin." Isaac Asimov says: "People who say *nauseous* for *nauseated are* nauseous!" But elsewhere he offers this bit of self-incrimination: "My own neologisms are always perfectly acceptable. It is those of others to which I object."

There are many other usages to which exception has been and is being taken. A few that come to mind are Bosley Crowther's "Screen Bests of 1964," President Kennedy's "So far as the new income tax laws, I'm for them," J. Edgar Hoover's "These kind of cases," the *Herald Tribune*'s "A Northport policeman had stopped Sallie Ann's car, after seeing she and her friend throw apples out the window at other cars," Merv Griffin's "There was a time when you couldn't used to say that," *The New York Times*' "Some students are repulsed by the thought of going into debt."

Other assorted criticisms of a general nature include confusion of *infer* and *imply*; mixups like *to draw a corollary between Trujillo and Sukarno*; pleonasms such as *he is very dead*; functional changes like that of *fun* in *fun time, fun dress, fun party*; the misuse of popular suffixes like *-wise*, which led an editor to admonish his cub reporter: "Wordwise, 'percentagewise' is unwise"; coinages like *sermonette*; alleged mispronunciations like CUE-pon; short cuts like *hopefully* for *in the hope that*.

Churchill, in accepting the *London Times* award for English literature, came out with his famous statement to the effect that the English language is the language of the redoubtable English-speaking peoples (than whom there was no whomer, in his estimation), and that we should preserve that language and see that it is not unduly damaged by modern slang adaptations and intruders. At this particular time he was shocked by such gobbledygook usages as *to quantify* and *in short supply*. But this praiseworthy attitude had not previously deterred him from coining the adjective *triphibious* and from satirizing purists who objected to prepositions at the end of sentences with the rejoinder, "This is nonsense up with which I will not put."

Henri Peyre of Yale, seeking to pinpoint the blame for the situation, wrote in the January 1963 issue of *Education in France*: "Some fanatics among descriptive linguists have even argued that correction in language is a superstition. . . . They decreed that all forms of speech, whether used in so-called polite society and among people who went to school, or picked up from the gutter and seasoned with scatology worthy of Céline or Henry Miller, are equal. . . . All syntactical forms are legitimized in this new freedom. . . . No literature should hold any preeminence over any other." Other critics have spoken of "the genius of the substandard speaker," of his sloppy, careless diction miscalled Americanese and featuring such gems as *Whaddya know?*, *Watcha have?*, *Doncha see?*, *Chadoon?*, *Joo see 'em?* The editor of the campus paper at Marshall University in West Virginia blames the students' mistakes on faculty members who confuse *except* and *accept*, say "Don't make no mistake about it," and misspell such words as *their, receive, believe, too, all right, separate, privilege,* and *definite*.

Rising to their own defense, some among the descriptive linguists are quite vocal. Robert A. Hall, Jr., not content with writing a whole book, entitled *Leave Your Language Alone!*, condemns all who offer advice on how to correct one's English as charlatans and quacks on a par with peddlers of cancer cures. More elegantly and convincingly, Bergen Evans, in a *Think* article of August 1959, points out that *like* for *as* appears in Shakespeare, Dryden, Burns, Shelley, Masefield, and Maugham; that *none* is construed with a plural verb in the King James Bible, which also does not hesitate to use double negatives, and that even earlier, Chaucer's Knight "didn't never do no villainy to no man." Marlowe is cited for his "Who have ye there, my lordes?" and Addison for "Who should I see there but the most artful procuress?" Finally, there is Noah Webster's flat statement: " 'Whom did you speak to?' was never used in speaking, as I can find, and is hardly English at all."

So much for the general situation. Several specific areas of language elicit specific criticisms. Foremost is the language of commercial advertising, which is held accountable for perhaps a major portion of the alleged degeneration of our language. The Madison Avenue tongue has a formidable rival in the gobbledygook of government circles, accompanied, aided, and abetted by similar forms of gobbledygook that prevail in the fields of science, education, and scholarship in general. That English is by no means alone in having these troubles is amply proved by the many books and articles that have been written abroad concerning similar phenomena appearing in French, German, even Russian. The rise of incomprehensible language forms in the scientific, scholarly, and administrative fields is perhaps a natural outgrowth of the multiplication of activities in those fields, and the consequent necessity of expanding an already overexpanded terminology to describe those activities. Nevertheless, the terminology tends needlessly to outstrip the need.

Other areas given critical scrutiny are the language of the press, the language of clichés and taboos, and, above all, what goes on in all the written forms of the language.

There is something more than haphazard growth and multiplication of forms in the written language. There is also an ideological conflict between those who view the written language as something sacred and superior to speech, and those who consider writing to be a mere Johnny-come-lately, an excrescence of speech, which is the only "true" language; in short, that we have to put up with written speech until something better comes along. The latter view is held by a good many descriptive linguists and is bolstered by the fact that something different, if not better, is actually coming along in the form of recordings and tapes, which permit speech to be "canned" for purposes of transmission at a distance or to posterity.

But the written language endures. In fact, it has never been so widespread as it is today. Literacy campaigns in backward areas of the world are fast bringing the blessings of reading and writing, such as they may be, within reach of populations that had never read or written before. In the more advanced countries, the written form of the language is altogether indispensable, as anyone knows who has been faced with signs in Cyrillic, Arabic, Hebrew, or Japanese.

Supporters of the written language range all the way from literary experts, who believe that literature, in written form, embodies the best of human thought, and that this medium should not only be retained but be enshrined and regarded with a respect and awe bordering on veneration, to practical-minded people who view the written language as a highly useful, even indispensable symbol of speech, in the same fashion that a check is a highly useful symbol of currency for purposes of commercial exchange.

Professor Sheridan Baker of the University of Michigan boldly states in a paper published by the Michigan Academy of Science, Arts and Letters in 1964: "I simply reassert a belief that has prevailed for centuries—until the new linguists came along about thirty years ago—when I say that the written language is far more valuable than the spoken." The corollary to this proposition is offered by Professor Max Marshall in his article "The Limits of Speech," published in 1965. After reasserting the superiority of writing over speech, he goes on: "They [the descriptive linguists] claim that a freedom of language which occurs in speech should be used also, though incidentally, in writing." The dictionary consultants mentioned above are asked in each case to give two separate judgments as to whether a given form is acceptable to them in speech and in writing.

Writing, of course, has its own peculiar problems of usage, which deal on the one hand with the relation of pronunciation to spelling, on the other with such things as punctuation, capitalization, paragraphing, and sentence division. These writing adjuncts attempt to duplicate in the written language the function of what the linguists call suprasegmental elements in speech—stress, pitch, intonation, juncture.

Typical of the first problem are widespread misspellings, even among supposedly educated people, such as *concensus* and *supercede*, *recieve* and *beleive*, *seige* and *feasable*, *food at it's best*; the confusion of *principal* and *principle*, *marital* and *martial*, *cavalry* and *calvary*. *Route* and *rout* are confused not only in spelling but in pronunciation.

The New York Times recently carried a report of the American Council on Education concerning replies by entering freshmen at sixty-one colleges and universities as to their career choices. The replies included the following: *sicology*, *denestry*, *metalergest*, *mathamatics*, *archetic*, and *psyciartrist*. Among the less scholarly goals were those of the *hosale sailsmen*, *augriculter*, *stewerdes*, *bussenius*, *airanatics*, and *piolet*; while one of the would-be scholars admitted to being *undesided*.

Regarding punctuation and other written symbols, some writers have pointed out that a misplaced comma in writing can be just as devastating as a misplaced spoken-language juncture or pitch. The descriptive linguists are fond of citing such spoken-language samples as "What are we going to have for dinner, Mother?" with the same pitch on *Mother* that would be used in "What are we going to have for dinner, chicken?" They also have such ear-catching phrases as "An iceman is a nice man," or "A light housekeeper is not a lighthouse keeper." Maxwell Nurnberg in his *Pleasures of Learning* shows conclusively that equally disastrous results can be achieved by misplacing a comma: "The Republicans (,) say the Democrats (,) are sure to win"; "The backers of Kennedy say their candidate will get 283 electoral votes (,) more than the number needed for election"; "We are going to eat (,) John (,) before we go on."

Strangely, some descriptive linguists object most violently to writing horrors sponsored by the compilers of *Webster's Third* and publishers' manuals. R. A. Hall, Jr., for instance, thunders out as loudly as I do at the atrocities perpetrated by the innovators against that useful written-language device, the hyphen. *Nonnational,* when my eye first fell upon it, conjured up visions of a verb *nonnate* with which I was unfamiliar; it took a few seconds to realize that this was only my old friend *non-national* in modern dress. One also wonders why *Teachers' College* is corrected to *Teachers College.* The unconvincing explanation here is that *Teachers* is used not in a possessive function (College of Teachers), but as an adjective. If this is the case, one wonders why the plural form is used, when *Teacher College* would represent normal usage. An extreme sample of abuse of the apostrophe was supplied by a serious newspaper: "A Supreme Court Justice, who's life has been threatened . . ."

Since the language of the press regularly comes in written form, it may be well to discuss it next. Objections to some of its abuses have come from one of its best known spokesmen, Westbrook Pegler. He deplores the use of *convince* for *persuade; presently* for *currently; headquartered; whom he charges slugged him, an estimated 65 persons, in an expected six hours,* and the perpetual omission of *the* and *and.*

But Pegler only scratches the surface. There are other objectionable features: for example, the use of headline English, lending itself to abbreviations that are actually distortions (like *Norse* for *Norwegian* and *Dominica* for *Dominican*

Republic), and which in any case confuse meaning and be-fuddle the reader. What would you make, for instance, of a headline that read: "Casualties from Cold Cut"? Would this mean that a cold cut infected with botulism was causing deaths? Or that casualties due to cold weather, or to a head cold, were diminishing? "French Official in Leningrad" could mean, conceivably, that the USSR now recognizes French as an official language along with Russian; it could also mean that an official from France had reached the Soviet Athens. "Madison Square Boys' Club" could lend itself to the interpretation that the members of the club are squares. "Black Bars Stay for Slayer" could mean that some "black bars" stayed behind awaiting a killer, as well as that Justice Black had turned down the killer's appeal. "Investing Clubs Weather Losses" leaves you in doubt about the function of the first three words. In all these cases, the fault lies partly with the headline writer, partly with the English language itself. Not too much can be done about the language; but the writers can no doubt do better.

Another criticism is directed at some columnists' overcrea‚ tivity. If you like their coinages—and I happen to—you will enjoy Sobol's *broilevards* for streets baked in New York summer heat, and Winchell's *complimention, pianostalgia, prosperaganda, artificivilization, booklegger, playsical,* and *eighty-eighting.* If you don't like them—and one of my editors loathes them—you will run a blue pencil through any mention of them. They are perhaps in the nature of nonce words; better yet, like Lewis Carroll's portmanteau words, they are words designed to carry two meanings in a single form. But they display ingenuity and creativeness, and they are the stuff that language grows by. Some of them fall by the wayside, others stay on. Who first coined *motel, smog, grismal?* What administrative genius first came out with *litterbug,* based on the analogy of an earlier *jitterbug?* It is interesting to note that when the New York City Transit Authority ran a contest to elicit suggestions of names for various types of rude passengers, such coinages as *jumboob, seat cheetah, hitting bull* (the names were supposed to represent animals and the content to encourage courtesy) failed to find fertile ground.

The language of comic strips normally appears in newspapers. It is therefore of interest to report that a *Newsweek* study of the percentage of distortions in various strips indicates that Palooka is the worst offender, with a score of almost 20 percent; Mickey Mouse is the runner-up; but Tarzan has less than 1 percent, and Henry a perfect zero. The study further shows that no fewer than sixty-nine words are used in comic strips to represent varieties of sound. Leading are *heh, haw, humm, grrock, pong, wagnity, yopple, wham, zip,* and *bing.* Carrying extra semantic content are *swell* and *gosh.*

Coming back to the spoken language, and before we take up in detail those three great areas of dissension—advertising, gobbledygook, and the language of the scholars and specialists —there is the matter of popular reaction to the language of clichés. Here again, surprisingly, we find some of the most authoritative descriptive linguists lined up squarely in the opposition ranks. Bergen Evans, for example, is loud in his denunciation of all clichés, despite the fact that he should favor them, since they superlatively represent popular usage. The clichés he objects to are mostly of the traditional variety, and this may have something to do with his attitude. What may not be generally realized is that new clichés are forever being formed and put into circulation. Quite modern, not to say ultramodern, are such cliché words as *to bug, bit, stacked, scram, swinger, vomitations,* the ineffable *camp* (defined as "acceptance of the odd as artistic," or "conscious defense of excessive mannerisms," and now accompanied by an adjective, *campy,* and an opposite, *stoop,* which is presumably an abbreviation of *stupid,* somebody or something who or which is not *camp*). There are cliché expressions favored by those who "think young"; *to have a ball, to have had it, to get with it,*

let's face it, it's the bomb, you can't do this to me, that's life.
There is a use of *-ville* not countenanced by our older dictionaries and ignored even by *Webster's Third*: *Phonysville, Squaresville, Moneyville,* even *Pukesville* and *Clichésville*. There is the new use of *standing up, straight up,* or just *up* for a drink of liquor that is not *on the rocks,* itself a cliché. There are strange uses reported from the campuses of women's colleges: *Hilda,* to mean "awful" ("What a Hilda day I had!"); *to read someone,* not in the military communications sense ("Do you read me?"), but in the sense of to bawl out someone in subtle, bitter, or sarcastic fashion ("Put him in his place! Read him!"); a use of the definite article with people's first or even family names (the Edward, the Jacqueline, the Jones), paralleling what often goes on in languages like French or Italian (*la Boncour, la Rosetta, il Petrarca*); even a use of the letter *x,* symbolized by crossed index fingers when speech is unavailable, to refer to anything Jewish (*an xy dress, Xland* for Israel, *no x's here*). Deplorable in thought and content as are some of these new clichés, they prove that the cliché is definitely a part of popular usage, and that an apostle of that usage has no business fighting the cliché.

Justifiedly first among the three major areas of specific criticism is the language of the advertising world. In his *Time Lurches On,* Ralph Schoenstein points out that the Refreshment Complex at the World's Fair is an example of the grandiose use of *complex* for any cluster of buildings. He goes on to discuss *marvelously young heel* for a nylon stocking, *thinking young* for soft drinks, but *thinking clean* for gas (he might have added *poorthink* for one who exercises Ben Franklin's quality of thrift, now much in disrepute, and even *Think* itself, used as an IBM slogan). *Gooder, deliciousest, the cleaningest, the now car,* and other assorted grammatical horrors come in for their innings, as does a tea that *psyches you up* and *Have a real cigar!,* as against the presumably imaginary cigars of the competitors. *Put a tiger in your tank!* has been improved upon by a Japanese brewer, who insists you "put a tiger in your tankard!"

The coinages of the advertising world have drawn much fire. They include such items as *floatel, roadability* (or *roadsmobility,* or even *Oldsmobility*), *coatability* (said to be the quality of coating the stomach lining), *pizazz, zoom, quadrapoise,* and *cruisomatic.* Among euphemisms designed to attract the unwary buyer are *wedding white, oversized room, gracious living, young moderns,* and *preowned* (for what used to be *secondhand*). Then there is the well-known series of pithy, three-letter names for products (Fab, Tab, Vel, Joy, All, Duz), occasionally expanded into a four- or five-letter word that must still be monosyllabic (Tide, Whisk, Charm, Gleem, Crest). There are the slogans: "whiter than white," "stronger than dirt," "refreshes you best," "Don't wait to be told," "Come alive," "We must be doing something right." "Mother, please! I'd rather do it myself!" aroused such guffaws of laughter that it had to be withdrawn quickly. A cat appears on TV screens and newspaper pages with this highly grammatical caption: "I've got nine lives; do you?" Another ad shows a big platter of Italian antipasto, properly labeled, and flanked by a mug of beer, for which the label is "antithirsto." Distortions of pronunciation run all the way from the subtle *Supp-hose* through the misplaced accent of "Come along with me to the wine coun-tree," to the wildly improbable Halo for Hello.

Studies of the language of advertising reveal that the six words most frequently used are *new, white, power, mild, refreshing, relief.* Runners-up are *enjoy, polls, news, switch, provocative.*

Probably more than any other type of language, that of advertising lends itself to the charge that language is being abused. In addition, it is all-pervasive. Like death and taxes, no one can escape it.

*   *   *

Much has been written about the language of officialdom, variously known as gobbledygook, Federal Prose, Washington Choctaw, Federalese, Officialese, and by a dozen other names. Characteristic traits of this language are that it never uses one short word when ten long ones will suffice, and that it enshrouds meaning in a cloud of verbiage worthy of some of our most noted authors of so-called literature. To this is added a proneness to coin words and expressions, a form of linguistic creativity that verges on mania.

Many explanations have been offered for this nature of Federal Prose, none completely satisfactory. One is that the obscurity of gobbledygook is designed to spread the responsibility for any action that the gobbledygook directive may involve, and to pass the buck until it is no longer passable (instructive in this connection is the story that Harry Truman had a sign on his desk: "The buck stops here"). Another account states that the nature of Federal Prose is a direct consequence of the fact that so many of its writers are academically trained and fancy themselves scholars (as will be seen shortly, the language of scholarship is traditionally and historically one of the worst offenders). A third theory is that gobbledygook stems directly from the language of the law, with its well-known archaisms and involvements. A fourth hypothesis is that the boys in government bureaus find time hanging heavy on their hands and simply amuse themselves in writing contests, with first prize going to the one who carries the art of befuddlement to its outer limits.

However this may be, here are one or two recent samples. From the Land Management Bureau comes this gem:

> The multifarious overlapping planning units have produced fragmented data, oriented toward single uses of land, exacerbating the problem. . . . Temperature is measured with the present accuracy of our knowledge of temperature effects on resources utilization, and provides us with a standard measurement which can be linked empirically to specific environmental applications.

An Army directive is accompanied by the following statement: "Dissemination of this directive will be restricted to key personnel directly concerned with the implementation thereof." While reasonably clear, that piece of gobbledygook lends credence to a belief that this is the scholarly mind at work; compare with a great university's slogan, "Man's right to knowledge and the free use thereof." "Its implementation" and "its free use" would have served the purpose as well.

Among vocabulary creations of gobbledygook we find: *to finalize, to definitize, to computerize, to orbitize, to delethalize, dismerger, categoring, framization, manpowerization, containerization,* even *interliaisation,* which leads a mocker to suggest further coinages on the stem of *liaison,* such as *to liaise, liaiser, liaisible,* and *laissez-liaiser.* While relatively few of the jewels of gobbledygook pass on to general use, we may point to *finalize,* above, as one that has made the grade. Another, now so widespread that it is no longer even noticed, is *breakthrough.*

While gobbledygook is an undoubted menace, it does not seem to warrant equal rank with the monosyllabic language of advertising. Gobbledygook is something to wonder at and admire, but it is not catching.

For the last of our specific divisions of language, the tongue of scholarship and education, we are faced with a dichotomy.

On the one hand, there are complaints about widespread ignorance and the use of slang terms and expressions, as betokened by the statement cited above of the editor of the campus paper at Marshall University to the effect that the language of the instructors was, if anything, worse than that of the students. Another testimonial comes from Professor Cameron Allen of Johns Hopkins, who claims that the ability to speak well is a liability rather than an asset, since people feel you are high-hatting them or being undemocratic if you don't sink to their level in your speech.

On the other side of the ledger is an article by John Fischer, editor of *Harper's Magazine,* entitled "Why Nobody Can't Write Good." Dr. Fischer states that, in the first place, a good deal of the blame for poor English standards must go to the schools of so-called creative writing, which teach their students to write so creatively that ultimately they find themselves in a class by themselves in spelling, punctuation, capitalization, sentence construction, and the use of words. Dr. Fischer goes on to examine the reverse of his medal, and discovers, a little belatedly perhaps, that there is a tradition in the academic world that a scholarly dissertation, to be scholarly, must be written not in plain English, but in that peculiar argot known as Pedagese or Academic Mandarin (Academese is another name for it). He offers no samples, but refers the reader to the pages of *PMLA (Publications of the Modern Language Association).* Finally, he deplores the fact that teachers and professors of subjects other than English no longer feel it is incumbent upon them to correct the English form of their students' reports, as they once did. The physics professor, in other words, is on the lookout for errors in physics, not in English, and the history man is concerned only with correct dates and happenings.

An even more comprehensive view of the situation appears in *Ohio State Newsletter* for May 1966, in which Edgar Dale gives a sample of an imaginary conversation between a young, innocent, and enthusiastic assistant professor and his superior, Dr. Maxim Kleeshay, who objects to the plain English used by the junior officer in his writings, and makes various constructive suggestions as to how a truly scholarly paper or book should be worded. Not only should the younger man learn the eternal truth that one short word should never be used where ten long ones will serve his purpose equally well; he is also instructed in the appropriate technical terminology: *challenges, ever-growing, ever-expanding, world in flux, critical thinking, constructive approach to a problem, basic fundamentals, desirable goals, evaluative criteria, vitalizing the teaching process.* All this must be liberally sprinkled with *must*'s and *interpret*'s; all objectives must be made primary; and *reorientation* must appear at every step (someone else has suggested that a Reorient Express be made part of the standard field equipment for scholarly courses).

The foregoing is only a mild sample of what goes on in the world of scholarship, where the most deadly charge that can be leveled at a writer is that he makes himself understood by the people to whom his writing is addressed.

The scholarly tradition of involvement and obscurity goes all the way back to the Middle Ages and the great philosophical disputes about how many angels could stand on the head of a pin. It may, however, be added that Academese, by its very nature, seldom spills over into the general language, and normally functions as a class jargon, similar to those of medicine, mathematics, and nuclear physics. It tends to invade the general language only in two areas, the fields of sociology and education. Since the aspects of this double threat are fraught with propagandistic features, designed to create certain states of mind and foster the acceptance of certain questionable practices, we shall reserve discussion of them for a later section.

At this point, after surveying the field and listening to the charges and the disclaimers, we may again formulate the question that appeared at the beginning of this chapter. Is the language being abused? Are all the manifestations, of which we have seen samples, to be accepted as inevitable and even desirable? Are they to be deplored, opposed, repressed, and suppressed? Are they part and parcel (one of the clichés to which Dr. Evans objects) of the natural growth and evolution of language? Are they in the nature of cancers or, at the very least, of warts on the body of language?

It may surprise most readers to be told that no matter what their reaction may be, there is not much they can do about the situation. It is the consensus of the speakers that determines the course of the language. If a great many speakers favor neologisms, distortions, and jargon, they will adopt them, use them, and so legitimize them. If not, these new forms will quickly disappear from circulation.

Esthetic and traditional arguments carry little weight in language. To argue that a form should not be used because it is esthetically unpleasant elicits the quick reply: "Unpleasant to whom? Who are you to tell me what I should and should not like?" To argue that it should not be used because it was not used a century ago is even more unreasonable. Lots of desirable things, and a few undesirable ones, did not exist a century ago.

Firmer ground is offered by utilitarian arguments. Language must be meaningful to be effective. Does a certain distinction between two words (*uninterested* and *disinterested*) establish a useful clarity of meaning? Again for the sake of clarity, is it preferable not to use the same word (*bimonthly*) for two contrary meanings? Avoiding confusion and misunderstanding is something to be sought after, on purely practical grounds. For the sake of practical understanding, there is a utilitarian argument on behalf of our knowing substandard language and recognizing it when we hear or see it. There may also be a utilitarian argument in favor of our not lapsing into it in the wrong milieus. *Webster's Third* is fully justified in recording all substandard usages; in fact, it may be criticized for not recording enough of them. But it is not justified in refraining from passing such value judgments as "substandard," "slang," "vulgarism," even "colloquialism," where such terms properly apply, not for the sake of snobbery, but for the guidance of its users.

WILLIAM F. MARQUARDT

The debate about whether or not language suffers from abuse probably antedates the Bible story in Judges that tells how Jepthah of Gilead and his followers slew at the fords of the Jordan forty-two thousand Ephraimites who pronounced the test word *Shibboleth* with an *s*.

The meting out of penalties to those who did not satisfy some standard of language behavior is frequently recorded in literature. The Spartan women in Aristophanes' *Lysistrata* were ridiculed for their dialect by their Athenian allies. Chaucer gently chides the nun in his Prologue to *The Canterbury Tales* because she spoke provincial French,

> After the scole of Stratford atte-Bowe
> For French of Paris was to hir unknowe.

and Captain Fluellen in *Henry V* fights, whips, and forces the English soldier Pistol to eat a leek for assuming that because he, Fluellen, "could not speak English in the native garb, he could not therefore handle an English cudgel" (Act V, sc.1, 11.75–76).

The ordinary man in ancient times felt that just as some kinds of language behavior were inferior to his there was also a standard of language behavior more or less out of his reach. If he was among the 90 percent of unlettered hewers of wood and drawers of wine of his society he did not worry much about his speech because he was expected to talk like his peers, not like his superiors, who gave orders and made the important decisions. If he or his son, however, because of talent or chance was given unusual responsibility he was also expected to make his language behavior fit the behavior required in the new role he was playing. With increasing knowledge, technology, and population, the number of persons concerned about acquiring new language behavior increased and this created a demand for manuals or grammars of linguistic etiquette.

These grammars had two bases: (1) the universal feeling among men and animals (but, according to the British anthropologist Geoffrey Gorer only among pack rats as intensely as among humans) that the behavior of members of one's own group is right and trustworthy, and of outsiders untrustworthy; (2) the belief that the nature of language had been defined and that the ideal behavior for any language group could be derived from proper authorities and taught.

The earliest extant Western treatises on language were not, however, written for pedagogical purposes. Certain dialogues of Plato written in the fourth century B.C. (*Cratylus*), Aristotle's essay *On Interpretation,* the writings of the Stoics, and the *Techne Grammatike* of Dionysius Thrax—all dealt with language as a subject for philosophical speculation, as a means of inquiry into the nature of being.

It wasn't long before the speculations of the Greeks became the prescriptive and proscriptive doctrines of the Romans and the teachers of language in the Western world. The categories and rules used to describe the Greek language—by scholars who showed no interest in other languages and whose term *barbaroi* for speakers of them is still with us in the English word *barbarians*—came to be applied to Latin. Since Latin and Greek were related in origin and had certain similarities in structure, the imposition of the model of Greek upon Latin was not the straitjacket that the model of Latin later proved to be for the vernaculars of Europe. But a notion that this imposition generated, namely that the model of language need not conform to everyday usage, paved the way for the notion that every language is governed by some abstract standard of correctness—a view still prevalent.

The Romans, however, were not oblivious to claims that usage should also determine propriety in speech. Aristotle's view that language was the product of convention and custom as opposed to the Platonic doctrine that language reflected immutable and eternal ideas was the basis for a continuing dialogue in which usage was accorded some attention. We see Horace saying in the first century B.C. in *De Arte Poetica*: "Use is the judge and law and rule of speech."

But the rhetorician Quintilian, writing several decades later in *Institutio Oratoria,* places constraints upon usage. He finds language to be based on "reason," "antiquity," and "authority" as well as on "usage." "Reason" finds its chief support in analogy and sometimes in etymology. "Antiquity" provides "majesty" and even "sanctity." "Authority" is derived from "orators and historians." Usage, although "the surest pilot in speaking," must be examined with "a critical judgment." It must not "be defined merely as the practice of the majority," for that would be "a very dangerous rule." In speech we should not accept "as a rule of language words and phrases that have become a vicious habit with a number of persons." Usage is therefore defined as "the agreed practice of educated men." [1]

The views of Quintilian have been cited repeatedly by grammarians from the days of the Roman Empire to modern times, and the influence of grammarians on the man of ordinary education is reflected in the words of Aulus Gellius in the second century A.D. in his *Attic Nights*:

Within my memory Aelius Melissus held the highest rank among the grammarians of his day at Rome. . . . Besides many other works which he wrote, he made a book which at the time when it was issued seemed to be one of remarkable learning. The title of the book was designed to be especially attractive to readers, for it was called *On Correctness in Speech*. Who

[1] Quoted by Karl W. Dykema, "Where Our Grammar Came From," in H. B. Allen, ed., *Readings in Applied English Linguistics* (New York: Meredith Publishing Company, 1964), p. 7.

then would suppose that he could speak correctly or with propriety unless he had learned those rules of Melissius?

The doctrines formulated by authorities like Quintilian and transmitted by laymen like Gellius but increasingly countered by a broader interpretation of the doctrine of the supremacy of usage expressed by Horace have been the basis for the continuing dialogue about language behavior. It has been suggested that the slow evolution of the concepts of democracy that have finally received expression in the latest civil rights legislation is analogous to a gradual acceptance of the legitimacy of usage as the arbiter of questions of propriety in language—an acceptance symbolized by the determined "nonprescriptive" stand taken by *Webster's Third New International Dictionary,* published in 1961. Since the appearance of *Webster's Third* coincided with the massive civil rights demonstrations of the Kennedy years, followed by the Civil Rights Act of 1964, the analogy is attractive to liberals in language matters.

But if there is any necessary connection between espousal of the political and economic rights and dignity of racial and social minorities and respect for all varieties of language, it is not obvious. We find a militant political liberal like Gore Vidal expressing vehement disapproval of *Webster's Third* and its new "scientific" attitude. Nor is it inconceivable that a staunch supporter of segregation in the South might be in favor of efforts to study and record all varieties of speech and make use of the findings in behalf of more effective communication among all groups.

Attitudes toward nonlinguistic behavior do, however, have a connection with attitudes toward linguistic behavior. As we come to see more and more that cultural behavior, like linguistic behavior, is communication, we begin to see that judgments as to the appropriateness of either type have something in common. Tying one's shoelaces, shaking hands, believing and denying, even breathing, when done in conscious ways in the manner of Hindu ascetics, are communicative acts in the context of the situation in which they take place. Linguistic behavior is after all a form of cultural behavior, and both can be evaluated by the same set of criteria. Using *ain't* in an English class is inappropriate in the same way, if not to the same extent, as whispering in church or laughing at a funeral. "Winston tastes good like a cigarette should," an advertising slogan, is susceptible to the same sort of judgment.

Having established that language behavior has much in common with other kinds, and that objections to certain language practices may derive from the same causes as objections to other kinds of behavior, we are ready to examine (1) the various kinds of language behavior objected to, (2) the persons associated with them, and (3) the persons who raise the objections.

Let us first say something about point 3 without exhausting the topic before dealing with it fully later. An interesting fact regarding complaints about language is that the persons guilty of the alleged "abuse" generally do not belong to the same group as the objector. The group may be different in point of geography, social class, occupation, age, educational background, religion, ideology, or cultural aim. The "abuse," furthermore, frequently affects the behavior of the group the objector belongs to or competes for the attention of other groups or of the general public.

The most widely deplored type of language "abuse" is that termed "bad grammar" and which comprises a well-known list of items of usage blacklisted in traditional grammars and condemned by teachers, writers, and persons thought of as guardians of the language. The criteria for admission to this list are vaguely specified. The items are alleged to be violations of various kinds: of a rule of Latin or of logic. Sometimes they are described as being illiterate, colloquial, or substandard; as archaic; as slang; or as finical or pedantic. The best known of such lists was compiled by Professor Sterling Leonard in the early 1930's for the purpose of testing the valuations placed upon 230 items of questionable usage by such varied users of language as linguists, English teachers, authors, editors, businessmen, language teachers, and teachers of speech.[2]

The verdicts of these diverse judges reflect wide disagreement as to the appropriateness of particular items for particular situations, but none at all as to whether submitting such items for evaluation to such a panel had any relation to improving general language behavior. When in 1938 Professors Albert H. Marckwardt and Fred Walcott examined each of the items in the Leonard survey with respect to its recorded usage in the *Oxford English Dictionary* and *Webster's New International Dictionary,* Second Edition, published in 1934, they found that the majority of the usages disapproved of by the judges in the Leonard study had been widely used by respectable writers over the course of time.

Persons studying language and its applications have been stating more and more frequently that the practice of watching for, listing, and condemning particular items of usage lifted out of the context of the situations in which they occur is, at best, meaningless as a way of bringing about effective language behavior and at worst harmful. This practice tends to make people more concerned about avoiding a condemned usage than about expressing meaning clearly and vividly, and more intent on listening for a condemned usage than on grasping meaning.

A type of language behavior that elicits little disagreement as to its being permissible in most situations is the use of taboo words. On this list are words of long standing, a few being among the most venerable words in the English language, as can be seen from the use of *shit* and *pisse* and other such terms by Chaucer's saltier Pilgrims, such as the Miller and the Shipman. The status of such words can be inferred from a statement by the lexicographer Eric Partridge: "F**k shares with c**t two distinctions: they are the only two stand-

2 Albert H. Marckwardt and Fred Walcott, *Facts About Current English Usage* (New York: Appleton-Century-Crofts, 1938), pp. 70–131.

ard English words excluded from all general and etymological dictionaries since the 18th century and . . . outside of medical and other official or semi-official and learned papers, still cannot be printed in full anywhere within the British Commonwealth of Nations." [3]

The taboo word, which encompasses a variety of expressions on the lower levels of slang, reflects man's perception of irrational or inexplicable forces within himself and in the world outside. It is a means whereby human beings can incite one another to sudden passion, fear, anger, or disgust. Taboo words comprise a small proportion of the total lexicon of any language and they vary in degree of revulsion they cause on their use in public. They belong to a limited subject area— invocation of the supernatural, reference to excretory functions, and reference to the sexual organs and sexual activities are among the most common. Use of them by the male within a small group is a sign of intimacy and if done with circumspection is accepted in most circles.

It can be argued that these words serve a genuine purpose. Human beings need an outlet for pent-up feeling, and they also need at times to jar others. The taboo word evokes a conditioned response. Used with calculation, it can be an instrument for getting quick attention or a powerful reaction, as the poet Howard Nemerov demonstrated at a Modern Language Association convention dinner in New York City in 1964. Early in his talk on contemporary poetry he tossed in the phrase "and all that shit." The rest of the talk bordered on the pedantic, but the audience remained wide awake till the end, expecting at every moment to be shocked again out of its complacency.

The total number of taboo words in an individual's lexicon appears to be fairly constant. Some belong to the basic word-stock of the language; others are as ephemeral as the impulse that gave them birth. The perennial ones are familiar to all

[3] Quoted by Gary Jennings, *Personalities of Language* (New York: Thomas Y. Crowell, 1965), p. 115.

members of the culture, though they are generally not uttered by modest women or by circumspect men in public. Although taboo words have their purposes, their effectiveness is in inverse proportion to how often they are used. Excessive use of them generally reflects a pathological urge to release tension rather than a need to carry on communication.

From widely condemned usages and taboo words we can move to a discussion of deviations from a standard by members of groups to which the objectors do not belong. The list of violations mounts as population increase and growth of specialization create more groups, as more persons become publicly articulate, and as technological development (the printing press, radio, telephone, television, and soon the videophone) makes these persons' expressions accessible to a large audience.

Merely to list the alleged language "abuses" would be unprofitable if it were not for the fact that they fall into four categories: those which allegedly (1) make language a less precise instrument for conveying meaning, (2) create in the minds of others false maps of reality, (3) aim at manipulating the minds of people for self-serving reasons, and (4) jar the sensibilities of the readers or listeners. A look at these four types of abuses and the persons generally accused of committing them should be illuminating.

The first type of abuse—that alleged to make language a less precise instrument for conveying meaning—has many varieties and perpetrators. One of the most common complaints in this category is directed at the use of words in senses different from their long-established or "basic" sense. Persons who deplore this kind of abuse are fond of repeating a few glaring examples. Among the most frequent criticism of *Webster's Third* was that it listed (and thus encouraged the use of) meanings that had not been associated with a given word in earlier times. For example: *shambles* as a scene of wreckage; *contact* as a verb; *transpire* to mean *happen*; *like* as a conjunction; *continuous* as identical with *continual*; *disinterested* as identical with *uninterested*.

The persons who deplore this type of abuse generally do so out of a belief that words have intrinsic or essential meanings rather than meanings contingent upon their contexts—syntactical, situational, and semantic.

Another type of abuse alleged to make language less precise is the use of multiple terms to express the same meaning. This complaint is most common in connection with the sciences or any field of expanding knowledge. The proliferation of terminology in the field of language study impels Professor Mario Pei to say in his *Glossary of Linguistic Terminology*:

> When *phonemic* can have a half-dozen synonyms; when the same type of sound change can be described by various writers as *combinatory, conditional, heteronomous, dependent, functional;* when one writer can use *prosodic* in the sense of *suprasegmental,* and another deny any identity between the two, it is not surprising that the student is confused. . . . There is perhaps need of an Academy of Linguistic Terminology, which will regiment and even repress ultra-creative flights.[4]

An abuse of language often charged to sociologists is that of creating neologisms. The well-known literary critic Malcolm Cowley, in an essay "Sociological Habit Patterns in Linguistic Transmogrification," [5] accuses them of liking "nothing better than inventing a word, deforming a word, or using a technical word in a strange context." Among the particular pleasures of the sociologist, according to Mr. Cowley, are (1) "making new combinations of nouns and adjectives and nouns used as adjectives," and "using complicated terms when there are simple ones available"; (2) using "nouns over all other parts of speech . . . in hyphenated pairs or dyads, and sometimes in triads, tetrads, and pentads . . . as adjectives

---

[4] Garden City, New York: Doubleday Anchor Book, 1966, p. vii.
[5] In Jack E. Conner and Marcelline Krafchick, eds., *Speaking of Rhetoric* (Boston: Houghton Mifflin Company, 1966), pp. 111 ff.

without change of form and . . . often . . . as verbs without the suffix " 'ize' "; (3) avoiding the use of pronouns, though "on rare occasions [calling] himself 'we' like Queen Elizabeth speaking from the throne, but . . . usually [avoiding] any personal form and [writing] as if he were a force of nature"; and (4) debasing the verb by "reducing" a transitive verb to an intransitive and avoiding the use of "transitive verbs of action" but using "verbs of relation, verbs which imply that one series of nouns and adjectives, used as the compound subject of a sentence, is larger or smaller than, dominant over, subordinate to, causative of, or resultant from another series of nouns and adjectives."

Charged with perpetrating similar abuses in recent news articles have been legislators, historians, and psychologists. A new manual prepared for the State of Connecticut General Assembly aims at giving "linguistic precision" to "the potentially pompous layman-lawmaker." He is told to use "void" in place of "null, void and of no effect" and "if" in place of "in the event that." [6] At about the same time Barbara Tuchman was warning a group of historians: "Let us beware of the plight of our colleagues, the behavioral scientists, who by the use of a proliferating jargon have painted themselves into a corner, or isolation ward, of intelligibility. They know what they mean but no one else does. Psychologists are the farthest gone in the disease and probably incurable."

Less noticeable but perhaps more prevalent abuses, and hence more dangerous, are clichés—"the con men of the realm of words," according to Robert B. Heilman, "the well-worn phrases that give the illusion of thought while actually interfering with thought." [7] Frank Sullivan in "The Cliché Expert Testifies on Crime" and similar *New Yorker* pieces demonstrates how newspapermen offend in this type of abuse. But the advertising man, the educator, the economist, and the politician have been equally charged with it and with

6 *The New York Times,* January 1, 1967.
7 "Freedom from Speech" in *Speaking of Rhetoric,* p. 61.

thereby keeping themselves and the communicatee from coming to grips with reality.

An offense similar to the cliché, one the politician is the most often charged with, is the euphemism, by which the harshness of reality is mitigated by the use of soft words. George Orwell in "Politics and the English Language" states: "Defenseless villages are bombarbed from the air, the inhabitants driven out into the countryside, the cattle machine-gunned, the huts set on fire with incendiary bullets: this is called *pacification*. Millions of peasants are robbed of their farms and sent trudging along the roads with no more than they can carry: this is called *transfer of population* or *rectification of frontiers*." [8]

Though the euphemisms can be found everywhere, H. L. Mencken shows how Americans in particular are addicted to elevating the status or image of jobs, objects, offices, or organizations by giving them impressive names or titles: *undertaker* becomes *mortician*; *real estate man* becomes *realtor*; *hairdresser* becomes *beautician*; *press agent* becomes *public relations counsel*; small colleges become *universities*; and in one city the garbage trucks are said to bear the legend "Table-Waste Disposal Department."

Akin to the euphemism as an alleged erosion of the precision of language are the "stale metaphors, similes, and idioms" which, in the words of George Orwell, "construct your sentences for you . . . think your thoughts for you . . . and conceal your meaning even from yourself." Political leaders promise to "leave no stone unturned," to "stand shoulder to shoulder" as they do their "epoch-making work."

The second category of alleged abuse, that which tends to create in the minds of users false maps of reality, first began to receive serious attention with the advent of "general semantics"—a branch of study ushered in by Alfred Korzybski in 1933 with the publication of his book *Science and Sanity*. The basic cause of this abuse, according to general seman-

8 In *Speaking of Rhetoric*, p. 29.

ticists, is the uncritical, almost universally held assumption that meaning lies in words. Related to this assumption is the failure to see that "the word is not the thing"—that the images words create and the reality they refer to are not identical.

From these misconceptions arises the failure to see that there are gradations in the abstractness of words extending from the concreteness of a word like *rattlesnake* to the decreasing concreteness of words like *predator* and *evil* and that the more abstract words become, the more they get meanings from "inside" the user rather than from "outside."

Thus the high proportion of words like *Communism, Americanism,* and *democracy* in our public dialogue, with their "intensional" meanings, tends to blur the picture of reality in people's minds. As technological development brings people into contact with more and more varied and unique experiences, the words and the meanings from which they get their maps of reality tend to create in them inner conflict and hence a greater sense of insecurity and restlessness.

Abuses of language that create distorted internal maps in people, usurping each person's own view of reality, have been charged to various groups. Advocates of our maintaining military preeminence have been accused of keeping alive such expressions as *defense, national security, balance of power, stalemate,* in order to keep the average person from studying the realities of nuclear weaponry and from seeing that security cannot result from the policies advocated and that in fact a large part of the military budget goes to maintaining forces in countries far from our own borders. President Kennedy in one of his speeches pointed out that terms—still used widely by defenders of the status quo—such as *free enterprise, the law of supply and demand,* and *balanced budget* no longer fit the economic realities of the 1960's. Russell Baker (*The New York Times,* January 29, 1967) points out that the terms *hipster, square, reactionary,* and *liberal* increasingly provide comfort to the classified as well as to the classifiers because they offer "a neatly prefabricated personality, complete with group opinion, group suit, group prejudice and even group manners."

Those most accused, however, of abusing language to bring about a reality different from that which people might otherwise live by are the advertising men. The language of the TV, magazine, and newspaper ad is designed to link the product with readily attainable comfort, efficiency, social acceptance, or self-esteem. One can easily become "a thinking man," one who "thinks young," "a man of distinction," one who'd "rather fight than switch," simply by buying what is offered. The language of advertising links Coca-Cola, razor blades, shaving cream, beer, cigarettes, bread, and spaghetti with a world full of domestic happiness, aristocratic elegance, rugged masculinity, and traditional American virtues. S. I. Hayakawa believes that the world created by the language of the TV ad among the Negroes of both the North and the South is the major cause of the intense civil rights agitation of the 1960's. The sharp contrast between the attempt through suggestive language to create a spirit of aspiration and belonging in every TV viewer, and the reality the Negro encounters the minute he leaves his TV set has given him a sense of frustration and despair that causes him to resort to any action, no matter how violent, to bring him nearer to the promise.

Abuses in the third category—those which bend the minds of people to a specific and limited reaction—are largely in the domain of advertising, but they are also being adapted to the needs of the politician, the government bureaucrat, the corporation executive, and the church leader. They attempt to make the listener or viewer, according to Franklyn S. Haiman, "buy, vote, or believe in a certain way by short-circuiting his conscious thought processes and planting suggestions or exerting pressures on the periphery of his consciousness which are intended to produce automatic, nonreflective behavior." [9]

Among the devices used to bring about such results are the use of testimonials ("20,679 physicians say 'Luckies are less irritating.' "); the use of misleading names and labels ("Uwanta" in imitation of "Uneeda"); blatant exaggeration (a food product—a "new discovery which adds solid flesh quick.")

With respect to the fourth category of abuses of language—those alleged to jar the sensibilities of readers or listeners—I will list from an infinite number only a few of the most chronic. Advertising is again the greatest offender: (1) the blatant use of sexual innuendo ("Does she or doesn't she? Only her hairdresser knows for sure."); (2) strident repetition of slogans; (3) mispronunciation of foreign names and expressions; (4) use of foreign words and expressions; (5) foreign accents in English speech on radio and TV; (6) use of slang or nonstandard speech; (7) clipping and slurring of speech by TV commentators at athletic events and by contestants in quiz shows.

It is clear from the foregoing examination of language as behavior that the features of language complained about are many. The various alleged abuses described above are only a few of the total number that have irked people at one time or another. And yet each offending word or phrase is sanctioned in some situation by persons other than the offender. Every utterance one produces naturally in his native tongue represents behavior patterns that "fit in" somewhere.

If this is the case, why is some language behavior or usage considered better than other behavior? Simply because it is believed to be behavior that would be practiced by most responsible and influential persons on that particular occasion. Is good usage then simply careful imitation of the

9 Franklyn S. Haiman, "Democratic Ethics and the Hidden Persuaders," in Richard L. Johannesen, ed., *Ethics and Persuasion* (New York: Random House, 1967), p. 59.

language behavior of an elite? No, because there is variety and flexibility in the behavior of such persons that makes "good" language behavior a matter of applying principles rather than mastering particular forms of language. Here are some of the types of variation that are available to a responsible user of language, from which he must be able to select on a given occasion or to which he must respond correctly. For convenience we will label them as variations of (1) time, (2) place, (3) social relationship, (4) register, (5) media, and (6) intention.

Variations of time result from the fact that language is constantly changing. New words, syntax patterns, and pronunciations appear every day, either to fit changes in the outer world, or to reflect changes in the attitudes of people. But older forms remain in the minds of persons who cling to them and in books and dictionaries. Archaic words like *whither, whence, milady, betake,* may for some persons seem less strange than newer ones that nevertheless sound out of date, such as *celluloid, roadster,* and *rumble seat.* And when we try to show reverence for the past on such occasions as religious ceremonies, rituals, and Fourth of July gatherings, we are disturbed if we do not hear a few forms such as *thou leadest, I thee wed,* or *city beautiful.*

Variations of place reflect the fact that where we live affects how we speak; in fact, many features of speech are inescapably linked to geographic area. To a limited extent we can, however, adopt features of language not our own to symbolize rapport with persons from other regions.

Variations of social relationship result from differing levels of intimacy people feel toward one another in communication situations. Attempts have been made to identify these levels, and the classification most frequently specified is a modification of one suggested by Martin Joos in his *The Five Clocks* (1962). They are: intimate (the patterns used between intimate friends and members of one's family); casual (patterns that imply rapport and mutual interest and provide very little background information); consultative (the language of small-group decision-making discussion in which background information is explicit and response is sought); deliberative (the language generally used in speaking to large groups in which delivery pace is regular, patterns are preplanned and somewhat complex, and response is not sought); oratorical (language in which the words, patterns, and manner of delivery have been carefully worked out to make the occasion seem memorable).

The fourth type of language variation—that of register—refers to the fact that the words and constructions plumbers use in talking shop are different from those electricians use, and that the lexicon and syntax that psychologists use in writing are different from those of the physicist.

Variations in language due to differences in media are those revealed in a comparison of speech with writing, or face-to-face conversation with telephone conversation or television delivery with lecture-hall delivery. As more and more persons are called upon to use these media, the differences in language behavior required for their successful use will be studied more carefully.

The sixth type of language variation—that due to intention—reflects such differing purposes as the desire simply to inform versus the desire to amuse, to awe, to inspire, or to convince. It comprises a wider range of differences than all the other types because it draws freely from them in giving uniqueness to such widely differing utterances as a limerick, an ode, a joke, or a political harangue.

Having surveyed a wide range of alleged abuses of language and also of the varieties available to the master communicator, we must now address ourselves to the question of whether it is possible to provide a definition of good usage. This is a task that has baffled many scholars. The most recent to try their hands are Neil Postman and Charles Weingartner, who assert: "good English is that which most effectively accomplishes the purposes of the speaker." [10]

Their definition caps a series of definitions they have reviewed and found wanting, particularly one by Robert Pooley, which has been much cited since the publication of his book *Teaching English Usage* in 1946:

> Good English is that form of speech which is appropriate to the purpose of the speaker, true to the language as it is, and comfortable to speaker and listener. It is the product of custom, neither cramped by rule nor freed from all restraint; it is never fixed but changes with the organic life of the language.[11]

In their effort to cut through verbiage, the authors of *Linguistics* ignore advice that they quote from I. A. Richards in the first chapter of their book—"a definition is a means of doing [something]"—and then painstakingly repeat: "In short, we must always bear in mind that a definition is an instrument which helps us do our thinking and accomplish our purpose." Since any definition of good usage is above all a way of guiding a speaker or writer on every conceivable occasion, it must serve him in times when he will not know the effect of his effort to communicate until long afterward—for example, when he speaks to a radio or TV audience—as well as when he receives immediate personal reaction. And it must also soothe his spirit when after his most earnest and carefully presented arguments at, say, a board of directors' meeting the vote is overwhelmingly against him.

It is time, then, to make one more attempt at a definition of usage that retains what is good in both the above definitions and at the same time helps a speaker or writer who is aware of the possible abuses and variations in language to say confidently what he has to say on any occasion:

> Good language usage reflects the communicator's adjustment to the expectations of the listener or reader, to his awareness of his own most effective manner, to his knowledge of the varia-

---

[10] *Linguistics* (New York: Delta Paperback, 1967), p. 94.
[11] New York: Appleton-Century-Crofts, p. 14.

tions of language appropriate for the occasion, and to his perception of whatever response he may receive.

The purpose of this new definition is to help every user of language communicate with zest, confidence, and empathy. But if it were widely adopted and seriously applied, it would also go far toward bringing to an end many of the complaints about the abuses of language.

Rejoinder : *Mario Pei*

Professor Marquardt does not carry through to a logical conclusion his point 1 (pp. 26-30): granted the existence of two words such as *disinterested* and *uninterested* (or *bimonthly* and *semimonthly*), with each pair matched by two different meanings—is it not a matter of both clarity and economy to restrict each word to a single meaning, rather than to confuse them, with consequent need for explanation? The context is not invariably self-explanatory (*bimonthly* and *semimonthly* payments are both legitimate).

Professor Marquardt's own definition of good language usage (page 38) makes such usage a matter of pure relativism, and altogether dependent on any given existing situation. Is there no such thing as "good language usage" *per se,* and valid in any conceivable situation? Does good language usage demand that I say "Them dogs is us'uns," if I am speaking to an Ozarks mountaineer, or "Dem guys is gonna be bumped off," if I am conversing with a big-city gangster?

Rejoinder : *William F. Marquardt*

Professor Pei's entertaining survey of the abuses of language invites paraphrase of Mark Twain's quip about the weather: "Everybody grousing about how people talk but nobody ain't doing nothing about it." Twain's quip was designed to provoke laughter among the gods. Its accuracy was not challenged—even though rituals to bring rain or to halt storms have been practiced in many societies since the beginning of time. Today, however, it sounds dated. Weather control is an established practice. *The New York Times,* on January 8, 1967, reports Secretary of the Interior Stewart L. Udall's announcement of "a vastly increased Federal program aimed at stimulating greater rainfall by 1972."

If control of the weather now seems a legitimate and attainable goal for society, control of language behavior must seem even more so. Professor Pei has long advocated language-behavior control. Witness his recommendation of an Academy of Linguistic Terminology, quoted in my article, and his urging that *Webster's Third* return to using such labels as " 'substandard,' 'slang,' 'vulgarism,' even 'colloquialism,' where such terms properly apply . . . for the guidance of its users." Professor Pei's suggested techniques, however, seem more analogous to the rituals practiced in times past for bringing rain than to those being currently employed by the Office of Atmospheric Water Resources of the Department of the Interior.

Elimination of the confusion and suffering caused by imperfections in the use of language in human affairs must come about in one or both of two ways: (1) the practice of self-discipline by all persons in the use of language through the educated application of basic principles, such as those suggested in my definition of good language usage; (2) application by "linguistic engineers" of techniques for modifying language behavior for socially desired ends discovered through surveys, collections of data, linguistic analysis, and experimentation.

Pursuit of the second way may reveal that many of Professor Pei's suggestions are sound, but they will then have scientific rather than primarily authoritarian sanction.

At any rate one of the first steps in a "linguistic-engineering approach" to the elimination of the imperfections in the use of language is a cataloguing of what all sorts of people consider "abusive" language. Professor Pei has made a start in that direction.

Chapter 2

English Spelling

MARIO PEI

When one considers the unbelievably illogical lack of connection between the pronunciation and the spelling of languages like English and French, one wonders how it ever
happened, all the more as there are plenty of other languages
where the relationship, or what the linguists call the "fit," is
much closer.

The major writing systems of the world are of two distinct
kinds. In the variety exemplified by Chinese, the written symbol represents not a sound but a thought-concept. Chinese
written characters work out quite like our written numerals.
If I write the figure 9, it will be natural for an English speaker
to read it "nine"; but a French speaker will just as naturally
read it *neuf,* a Spanish speaker *nueve,* a Russian speaker
devyat'. The written symbol conveys the same meaning to all
people who use Arabic numerals, no matter how much their
spoken rendition of 9 may differ.

It will be noted that this has advantages and disadvantages.
There is internationality of meaning when you use this system (called pictographic, ideographic, or logographic; that is,

the writing of pictures, of ideas, of words), and this is an un-doubted blessing. Chinese dialects, such as Mandarin and Cantonese, are in reality different spoken languages, and the speaker of one cannot understand the speech of the other; but he can read his written message with relative ease.

On the other hand, there is no portrayal of the sounds of the language you are using. If I see French written *neuf* or Spanish *nueve,* I can at least make a stab at pronouncing them, even though I may not know French or Spanish; but if I see the written Chinese character for 9, it will help me not at all with the spoken form. In fact, there are people who, in learning Chinese, concentrate exclusively on spoken forms, and there are others (translators of technical and diplomatic documents, for instance) who concentrate on the written char-acters and their meanings, and utterly disregard their spoken values.

The systems in use in the West, of which our own so-called Roman alphabet is typical, are phonetic, at least in principle. The written symbols (letters and combinations of letters) are meant to portray not meanings but sounds. In the case of short, simple words, this works out quite well; in the word *net* each of the three letters represents a separate sound, *n-e-t.* The three sounds, pronounced in rapid succession, give us a word that has a meaning to English speakers.

It is more than likely that when phonetic writing began, a real effort was made to correlate written symbols with spoken sounds. But difficulties appeared almost at once. The people who devised the first phonetic alphabets (Semitic-speaking Phoenicians) did not have the technical skill of modern lin-guists in analyzing and classifying language sounds. This led to certain initial confusions and omissions. By reason of the structure of their language, the Semitic alphabet makers thought it was unimportant to record vowel sounds, and produced an initial alphabet consisting only of consonants (something as though we were to write "H wll nt cm t fv bt t nn" for "He will not come at five but at nine"). Secondly, as the alphabet system was passed on to speakers of other languages, it was modified to suit the structure of the borrowing tongues (the Greeks, for instance, taking over the Semitic alphabet, deemed the vowel sounds worthy of inclusion, and arbitrarily changed the value of some Semitic consonant symbols to represent vowel sounds). As this borrowing spread from group to group the modifications, and also the inconsistencies, multiplied. In some cases the borrowers, having in their language sounds that did not appear in the language they borrowed from, created new symbols; in other cases, they represented the unrepresented sounds by combining old symbols, or by putting some sort of distinguishing mark over, under, or beside one of the original symbols.

Still another difficulty soon appeared. The sounds of spoken languages tend to change in the course of time. But once the writing system, or alphabet, has become set, there is a natural reluctance to make the change in writing that is beginning to appear in speech, with the result that the written form of many languages lags far behind the times. At one point in their history, the Romans pronounced *c* in all positions as *k*. At a later date, *c* before *e* and *i* changed in pronunciation to *ts* or *ch*, while it continued to be pronounced as *k* elsewhere. Ultimately, Latin *casa* and *centum*, in both of which *c* had originally the value of *k*, became Italian *casa* and *cento*. Because of reluctance to change the spelling, the same *c* symbol represents *k* in *casa*, but *ch* in *cento*.

This matter of hanging on to a traditional spelling that no longer reflects the pronunciation has some curious side features. Generally speaking, the European languages that achieved a literary form at an early date (English, French, to a much lesser degree Spanish and Italian) are the ones that offer the greatest inconsistencies; those that achieved it later (Hungarian, Finnish) have a far better fit between pronunciation and spelling. This is simply because the time spread was shorter in the case of Hungarian and Finnish, and the spoken languages had less time to change after the written form was achieved. There is also the question of how intrinsically conservative or evolutionary a language is in the matter of sound change. English and French, for historical reasons, have shown a far greater tendency to rapid and drastic sound change than Italian or Spanish.

English, originating as a mixture of West Germanic dialects spoken by the Angles, Saxons, and Jutes, was at first written in a Runic alphabet of twenty-four letters. Runic was a system of writing supposed to have been borrowed from the Greek, and used, with local variations, by most of the ancient Germanic tribes, particularly in Scandinavia. Anglo-Saxon inscriptions in Runic appear on English soil on memorial stones, tools, and coins. With the conversion of the Anglo-Saxons from paganism to Christianity came the gradual replacement of Runic with the Roman alphabet of the missionaries. Interestingly, a few of the old Runic characters were retained, notably *thorn* (þ), to represent the *th* sound which did not appear in Latin and was therefore not represented in the Roman alphabet; *wen*, representing the *w* sound which Latin no longer had; and ʒ, which originally had the value of hard *g*, but later turned into *y* before front vowels. (Front vowels are vowels articulated in the front part of the mouth, such as the *e* of *met* or the *i* of *machine*.)

There is no reason to suppose that the system of writing used by the Anglo-Saxons at the time of King Alfred differed greatly from its spoken counterpart. Some pronunciation changes were already under way, however, and, by reason of traditionalism, spelling began to lag behind. For instance, *f* between vowels had changed to *v*, so that the spelling *drifan* now betokened a pronunciation *drivan* (actually this becomes *drive* in modern English). The letter symbols þ and ð both appear in Anglo-Saxon, but instead of being logically specialized, one for the unvoiced *th* of *thing*, the other for the voiced *th* sound of *this* (as they are in Icelandic), they were generally interchanged. There is evidence that *c* and *g* in certain positions were already assuming the palatal sounds heard today in *churl, bridge,* even though the spelling continued to be *ceorl, brycg.* Traditionalism in spelling was a factor, even before the coming of the Normans, which revolutionized completely the sound-and-spelling picture.

The Normans, though of Scandinavian (and therefore Germanic) origin, had given up their ancestral Norse language, and by 1066 were speaking Old French, a language that had evolved out of Latin, but that was still quite different from the modern French of today. As Anglo-Saxon and Old French began to mingle, many peculiarities of Old French orthography were passed on to English. Anglo-Saxon had made practically no use of the letter *k,* using instead *c* in all positions with that value (*cniht, cyning,* where modern English has *knight, king*). Old French, on the other hand, made use of *k,* particularly before *e* and *i,* where Latin *c* had acquired the value of *ts* or *s.* Transmission of the letter *k* from Old French to English was in the nature of a desirable phonetic reform. Unfortunately, it was not consistent. Some English *k* sounds got to be spelled with *k* (*knight, king, ken*), but others retained the old Anglo-Saxon *c* (*call, cow, cold*). On the other hand, Old French used the combination *ch* with the value it has today in English *church,* and this combination was passed on to English, so that *ceorl* became *churl* and *cinn* became *chin.* The French combination *qu* replaced Anglo-Saxon *cw,* so that *cwēn* became *queen.* The old Runic letter *wen* was replaced by Norman-French *w,* and Runic þ and ð by Norman-French *th.* The "long *i,*" or *j,* was also a Norman importation. So was the insertion of a silent *u* after *g* in words like *tongue* and *guest.*

Despite all these innovations in the writing system, once it became stabilized it turned fairly phonetic. Chaucer's writing, for example, is a passable representation of the pronunciation of his period provided you do not insist on pronouncing the words modern fashion, but rather as you would pronounce them in a language like German or Italian. When Chaucer spells *droghte,* the pronunciation is DROKHteh, not as in modern *drought.* For the many new French words that had entered the language, the pronunciation was still that of Old French, and Old French, unlike it modern descendent, used reasonably phonetic spelling.

The regularization and standardization of spelling began (but it was a very modest beginning) under William Caxton, greatest of early English printers. Caxton's major contribution was perhaps that he consistently used in his printed works the London dialect (at his period, East Midland dialect would have been a better description). Before his time, writers had been in the habit of composing their works in their own native dialects, and since these were many and strikingly different, the spellings used diverged widely. But the artisans of the new art of printing also tended to be arbitrary and suit their own convenience, cutting down or amplifying words to match line requirements. *Gest, geste, gueste, ghest, gheste,* were all variant spellings of *guest* at this period. *Strayt* and *straight, tongue, townge,* and *toung, been, bin,* and *beene* all appear.

Between the Chaucerian and the Elizabethan eras, two major phenomena affected the relationship between sound and spelling. One was the insertion of etymology into spelling at the expense of fit. By natural processes of spoken-language change, Latin *debita* and *dubitare* had turned into French *dette* and *douter,* with complete elimination of *b.* The French words had passed into English in the forms of *det* or *dette* and *dout* or *doute.* Now scholars, both in France and England, suddenly became aware of the Latin source of their modern words. Since the parent language, Latin, which they venerated, had *b* in both words, ought not the *b* to be restored in their modern descendants, at least in writing? So both French and English began respelling their words as *debte* and *doubte* (*doubter* in the case of French). In English, most of these silent, etymological letters stuck. In French, they were partly eliminated at a later period. The result is that today English has *debt* and *doubt*, with a *b* that was never pronounced save in Latin, while French has gone back to the more phonetic spellings *dette* and *douter*.

Far more important, since it affected speech as well as writing, was the major transformation of English spoken vowel sounds that is still known among language scholars as the "Great English Vowel Shift." In Chaucer's time, as in Anglo-Saxon, English had long and short vowels. The long vowels were really what the name implied, pure vowel sounds that never changed quality while they were being uttered. Long *a* was the *a* of *father*, never the *a* of *late*. Long *e* was a sound best exemplified by modern German *zehn*. Long *i* was the *i* of *machine*, never the *i* of *bite*. Long *o* was again best exemplified by referring to German *ohne*. Long *u* was the *oo* of *pool*, never the *u* of *union*. These sounds were all pure, without any trace of the *y* and *w* glides that characterize the modern so-called long *a* of *bale* or long *o* of *sole* (note that if *bale* were spelled *bayle*, and *sole* were spelled *sowle*, the pronunciation would be exactly the same; a glide is a *y* or *w* sound immediately preceding or following a full vowel sound, as in *yard, ward, boy, low*).

As the true long vowels of Chaucer's day rearranged themselves in speech, a word like *bite*, which had been pronounced BEETeh, began to shift to its present pronunciation, turning its stressed pure long vowel into a diphthong. On the other hand, original diphthongs like the *ea* of *each* and the *oa* of *boat* tended to become pure vowels, then to turn once more into diphthongs, but with a different coloring. The spelling, however, had by this time become traditional, and was retained. Today, at least four of our five so-called long vowels are phonetically diphthongs (*i* of *bite, o* of *note, a* of *late, u* of *union;* some linguists claim that even the "long *e*" of *mete* is a diphthong, consisting of short *i* followed by a *y*-glide).

Along with all this, final *e*'s, which in Chaucer's time had been pronounced, turned silent, but continued to be written.

In fact, Mulcaster, a late-sixteenth-century grammarian, tried to put them to good use by proclaiming the principle that a silent final *e* at the end of a word should indicate a preceding "long" vowel. This accounts for such spellings as *made* where earlier writers had used *maad*.

Add to this the force of analogy, or imitation, whereby silent *gh*'s were inserted into words like the earlier *deleit* on the ground that since they had the same pronunciation as *night* and *light* they should be similarly spelled. But *night* and *light*, of Anglo-Saxon origin, had previously been pronounced NIKHT and LIKHT, and the *gh* represented a sound real enough historically, but later lost; *deleit* (or *delight*, in its new spelling), on the other hand, of French origin, had at no time a *kh* sound.

By the time of Shakespeare and the King James Bible, both pronunciation and spelling had settled down into what might be styled equal but separate grooves, not too unlike those of today. But the damage was done. The drastic sound transformations of the earlier periods had turned spoken English into a language quite dissimilar from that of Chaucer, let alone ancestral Anglo-Saxon. The traditional conservatism of some spellings, the irrational transformation of others, had forever severed the link between speech and writing.

Today we are faced with a language in which the letter combination *-ough* can have at least seven different values (*dough, bought, bough, rough, through, trough, hiccough*), while the sound most frequently represented by the combination *sh* (as in *shoe*) can also be represented by such spellings as *s* (sure), *ss* (issue), *si* (mansion), *ssi* (mission), *ti* (nation), *ci* (suspicion), *ce* (ocean), *se* (nauseous), *sci* (conscious), *ch* (chaperon), *sch* (schist), *chsi* (fuchsia), *psh* (pshaw). Silent letters abound (*b* of *plumb*, *p* of *pneumatic*, *ph* of *phthisic*, *g* of *gnaw*, *k* of *know*), while other letters and combinations are wrenched out of their normal rendition (*o* of *women*, *l* of *colonel*, *th* of *Thames*). You can't pronounce a spelling like *tear* until you get it in a context, while *meat, meet,* and *mete* are all pronounced alike, regardless of context or meaning.

It is somewhat to our credit that the last partly successful attempt to bring spelling in line with pronunciation was made by Noah Webster, in his *American Dictionary* of 1828. It was he who gave us such semiphonetic spellings as *honor, center, traveler, program, check, draft, defense, plow,* as against the still current British spellings *honour, centre, traveller, programme, cheque, draught, defence, plough.*

Since his time, there have been plenty of attempts to continue the reform of spelling to bring it in line with pronunciation. Some are of commercial origin (*thru, tho, Starlite, burlesk, sox*), others stem from certain reform-minded newspapers (*burocracy, demagog, thorobred, midrif, lexicografer*). They have not met with general acceptance. Traditionalism is far too strong. A person who has invested countless hours and endless labor learning to spell irrationally has an unconscious vested interest in the irrational system once he has mastered it, and no amount of argument on behalf of ease to his descendants will shake him.

There is, of course, far more than sheer pigheadedness and selfishness at work. It has been repeatedly pointed out by opponents of spelling reform (1) that if we were to phoneticize our spelling, all of our tremendous stock of written and printed material would have to be reissued in the new spelling, a process that would take decades, in the course of which the pronunciation might well undergo new changes calling for additional reforms; (2) that in the meantime, people, to be thoroughly literate, would have to learn both systems; (3) that such a process would involve extensive material changes, such as the retooling of all our linotype machines and typewriters, and the retraining of their operators, who through great effort have learned to operate them in their present form to the point where the operation has become automatic; (4) that there would have to be an extensive revision of our dictionaries; *nation* and *national,* for instance, would no longer appear together, since the first *a* of *nation* represents a different sound from the first *a* of *national;* (5) that such advantages as we now reap from etymological spelling would be lost; any speaker of a Western tongue now recognizes *nation* in written form; he would no longer recognize it if it were spelled [nejʃən], as in International Phonetic Alphabet (IPA) characters, or in one of the many reform spellings suggested (*naeshun, neysheun*). As against all these disadvantages there would be the undoubted saving of time and money involved in teaching both our schoolchildren and foreigners who want to learn English how to link our present spelling with our present pronunciation.

This is where the matter rests today. It may be added that any attempt to phoneticize the language would have to be preceded and accompanied by an even more difficult attempt to standardize the spoken tongue. The spread in spoken form between British and American English, not to mention the various regional dialects of both, is such that if it is not first eliminated we will wind up with a series of different phoneticizations, all equally correct and valid, in the sense that they all represent authentic pronunciations, but so divergent as to cause endless confusion. Is the game worth the candle?

It may be of interest to survey briefly what happens in other languages, in the matter of spelling reform. French is the only major Western language in which the spread between pronunciation and spelling even remotely approaches the English situation. In French, however, the rules governing the relationship between the two items, while quite lengthy and complicated, nevertheless exist. Barring a large but limited number of exceptions (*cuiller, aiguille, second,* pronunciation of final *-s* in such singular noun forms as *sens, ours, os,* and such plural noun forms as *moeurs,* a few special verb forms such as *j'eus*), it is possible to establish the pronunciation from the spelling, though not the spelling from the pronunciation. French spelling received its last general going over at the hands of the French Academy in the early part of the nineteenth century, and has since then remained stable. There is no widespread movement to phoneticize it, beyond the use of phonetic and phonemic transcriptions for scientific purposes. The French seem content to let their archaic and unphonetic spelling stand. Certain pronunciation changes are occurring in spoken French at the present time (merger of *a* and *â*, of *in* and *un*, uncertainty as to the degree of openness of certain vowel sounds in final position, as in *j'aimerai* and *j'aimerais*), but these do not seem to give rise to excessive confusion so far as native speakers are concerned. It must, however, be acknowledged that French offers almost as large a number of homophones (words differently spelled and of different meanings, but pronounced exactly alike) as does English. The phonetic transcription [sã], for example, can be represented in writing by *cent, sans, sang, s'en, sent, (Georges) Sand;* [ɛme] can represent *aimer, aimez, aimai, aimé, aimée, aimés, aimées.* Silent etymological letters at the end of words cause further confusion (*lac, donc,* vs. *clerc, jonc*). So does *liaison,* the linking of otherwise silent final consonants to the initial vowel sound of the following word (*ils* is normally pronounced [il], but in *ils ont* the *s,* pronounced as a *z,* is carried over to *ont* and pronounced with it [il zõ]). The very same objections that arise in connection with spelling reform in English are operative in the case of French.

Spanish offers few difficulties of spelling and pronunciation. Chief among them are silent initial *h* (*ha, a*); the confusion of written *b* and *v,* where spelling usually follows etymology but the pronunciation has redistributed itself so that either letter, initially or after consonants, is pronounced *b,* but between vowels is pronounced as a bilabial *v.* In certain non-Castilian areas, there is confusion between *ll* and *y* (la Jolla, in California Mexican speech, is equivalent to *la joya*); locally, there is confusion between *s* and *c* before *e* or *i,* and *z* (*casa, caza,* distinguished in Castilian speech, sound alike in Cuba). These are minor troubles, and there is no general movement to reform Spanish spelling, which became set in its present form about two centuries ago. No notable pronunciation changes are in progress, except for a few localisms.

Italian, in its standard national form, gives rise to very little confusion, generally limited to the use of silent *h* (*ho, o; hanno, anno*); the use of *h* to indicate velar pronunciation for *c, g, sc* before *e* and *i* (*chi, ghiro, scheletro*), and of *i* to indicate palatal pronunciation for *c, g, sc* before *a, o, u* (*ciao, giara, sciopero*). (A velar is pronounced in the back of the mouth and involves the velum, or soft palate; an older and more popular synonym is "guttural.") The open or closed pronunciation of stressed *e* and *o,* not indicated in writing, occasionally lends itself to confusion (*pesca* with open *e,* "peach"; *pesca* with closed *e,* "fishing"). Italian offers difficulties to foreign learners (but seldom to natives) by not indicating the position of the stress except in final position (*città, virtù*; but *rapido,* RAHpeedoh; *pecora,* PEHkohrah). No perceptible movement for reforming spelling is in existence.

German orthography lends itself to few misunderstandings, though the use of a double consonant after a vowel, which normally betokens a short value for the vowel, is occasionally misleading (*lassen,* with short *a*; but *stossen,* with long *o*). The tendency in present-day German is to use Roman both in print and in script, rather than the traditional Black Letter, or Gothic, alphabet, and the angular *Fraktur* handscript. There is a less marked tendency to eliminate capitalization of common nouns (*brot* instead of *Brot*); Danish and Swedish gave up the practice quite some time ago; it was occasional even in seventeenth- and eighteenth-century English. No notable pronunciation changes are in progress, nor is there any organized spelling-reform movement.

A good deal has been heard about orthographic reform in Russian and Turkish. Reform in the former consisted largely of the elimination of certain letters in the Russian Cyrillic alphabet that had historically merged in pronunciation with other letters, or had become silent. Beyond that, the Soviet reformers made no attempt to improve the phonetic representation of the sounds of the Russian language, which still presents a large number of confusing features (*g*, for example, is pronounced *v* in certain case forms; written vowels, notable *o*, may have different sounds in different positions in relation to the accent; certain palatal consonants affect the pronunciation of following vowels in ways that are not reflected in the spelling; above all, there is no written indication of where the unpredictable word-stress falls). Despite all this, there is no organized movement further to phoneticize written Russian.

For Turkish, spelling reform consisted in shifting over from the unphonetic Arabic alphabet to the Roman, something not too difficult to accomplish in a country that was at the time 80 percent illiterate and without too large a stock of written and printed matter. Since the shift occurred early in our century, and there was no weight of tradition to be coped with, it was possible for the reformers to achieve a highly phonetic rendering of modern Turkish sounds. The "fit" of Turkish is excellent, as is that of other languages that achieved their written form in relatively recent times (Finnish, Hungarian, Indonesian).

A good deal is made of the so-called spelling reforms that are periodically carried on in such languages as Norwegian and Portuguese. In Norwegian the reform is aimed not so much at phoneticizing the language as at differentiating it from the Danish, which was at one time official in Norway. For Portuguese, a great deal could be done, but is normally overlooked by Portuguese-Brazilian commissions, which concern themselves with very minor points, such as the use of accent marks to indicate open or closed quality for vowels. One of the major achievements of the reformers, however, was the elimination of written double consonants that are not pronounced double or stressed (*janela* for older *janella*, *sêco* for *secco*). But Portuguese, like English, Russian, and other

languages, is a tongue in which identical vowels have traditionally assumed different sounds in different positions, and
this is only occasionally brought out by the spelling (*Macau*
for an older *Macao* is one of the rare samples). Again it must
be stressed that any attempt to render phonetically present-
day Portuguese-Brazilian pronunciation would run into the
same difficulties that appear in English.

For languages like Chinese and Japanese, the process of
phoneticization is in an altogether different category. Here it
is a matter of shifting over from a writing system that symbolizes objects, ideas, and concepts to one that symbolizes
spoken language sounds. While such phoneticization is usually linked to Romanization (that is, the use of the Roman
alphabet in a phonetic way), this link is not at all essential.
Phoneticization of the ideograph-using languages could just
as easily (perhaps more easily) be effected with the use of IPA
characters, or with a different alphabet, like the Cyrillic (in
fact, for a time the Communist Chinese orthographic reformers toyed with the idea of using modified Cyrillic characters). Preference for the Roman alphabet in this connection
hinges on its widespread use rather than on any intrinsic
superior merits.

The movement toward phoneticization in China has the
official endorsement of the Chinese Communist Party, but is
apparently to be carried on simultaneously with a reform of
the system of Chinese characters designed to make the latter
easier to use and more accessible to the masses.

In Japanese, the *Romaji* movement has been in existence
for a very long time, and Japanese appears frequently in a
highly satisfactory Roman-alphabet transcription which is not,
however, official. The difficulties in the way of making a phonetic Roman alphabet universal in both countries, to the
exclusion of the ideographic system, are attended by the
usual objections: existence of a large body of literature in
ideographic characters that would have to be gradually re-

placed, and violation of a centuries-old tradition that is a deeply rooted part of the Chinese and Japanese cultures.

Shifting back to our own problems, two radically different approaches are now widely used to facilitate the process of learning to read and write for the younger English-speaking generations. One is the so-called Phonic approach, used with some success in a number of American school systems. This consists, basically, in setting up a rather large number of rules (to which, however, there are still far too many exceptions) that purport to govern and illustrate the relationship between the spoken and the written form. The idea goes all the way back to Mulcaster, who in the late sixteenth century, as we have seen, tried to establish such general principles as the one that a vowel followed by a single consonant followed in turn by unpronounced *e* is "long" (*made, late, bite, lone, rule*); but a vowel followed by one or more consonants and no *e* is "short" (*net, bit, mat, lot, risk, list, last, ask*). Special subrules are formulated to take care of consistent exceptions (*find, bind, rind, mind*; or *night, light, bright*: in a final *-ind* or *-ight* group, *i* is "long"). The trouble with Phonics is the very large number of exceptions and inconsistencies for which no rule can be formulated or applied. In a sense, it might be said that the principle underlying Phonics is that of making the spoken language fit into the written. This makes Phonics anathema to descriptive linguists, who believe that everything should start from the spoken form.

The opposite principle, that of making writing fit into speech, is shown by the Augmented Roman Alphabet, also called International Teaching Alphabet (ITA), devised by Isaac Pitman, and used in many British schools as an initial device to teach children to read and write. Here a sort of semiphonetic alphabet consisting of a larger number of characters than the twenty-six of the ordinary Roman is used, and the children fall rather easily into the practice of reading and writing in it, since its symbols approximate the sounds of speech. Once they have learned to use Augmented Roman, they are shifted over gradually to traditional spelling; but by this time they have already acquired the reading and writing habit, and the adjustment is easier than it would be if both the reading and writing process and the inconsistencies of our normal spelling were presented at the same time.

Both systems have undoubted merits, but neither basically solves the problem of the monstrous spread between the written and the spoken forms of English.

It is difficult to formulate any sort of sensible solution. In the abstract, spelling reform is an extremely simple matter. All we have to do is to select a system of written symbols that will represent on a one-to-one basis the significant sounds, or phonemes, of the spoken language, and offer it to our younger generations. But in practice, we are faced with the fact that so-called generations do not come in compartmentalized units, but have to work with one another. They overlap, even while they differ in mentality and outlook. Whereas a younger person will find it quite natural to take a plane to his destination, an older one may shrink from the experience, and prefer the railroad train to which he became accustomed in his youth, even though it takes longer. A very old person may even shrink from riding in an automobile. While a younger person finds it quite natural to get his news reports and entertainment from TV, the older may prefer the traditional newspaper and books. But all these people are alive at the same time, and have to mingle.

In principle, it would be much simpler if we of the English-speaking world gave up our antiquated system of measurements and weights (inches, feet, yards, miles; pints, quarts, gallons; bushels, ounces, pounds; Fahrenheit degrees), and shifted over to the absolutely regular, scientific decimal system (centimeters, meters, kilometers; liters, grams, hectograms; Centigrade degrees, with zero for freezing and 100 for boiling, instead of a highly arbitrary 32 and 212). But industry informs us that it would take many billions of dollars in retooling to shift over from our present system of measurements to the scientific one. Calendar reform is in principle highly desirable: thirteen months of twenty-eight days each, with an extra day for New Year and two for leap years. How much confusion would be saved if Monday invariably fell on the first, eighth, fifteenth, and twenty-second day of each month! An international currency would solve endless problems of foreign exchange, though it might work havoc with the economies of some weaker nations. An international language would be highly desirable, though it would tread on many nationalistic cultural toes.

But tradition is something that must be reckoned with. Whatever our anthropologists, socialists, and other reformist do-gooders may say, it is utterly impossible to reshape man and his thoughtways overnight. Change must be gradual to be psychologically effective. Furthermore, real, hard, material objections often stand in the way of what looks at first glance like a highly desirable change. For spelling reform these have been enumerated, and seen to be formidable.

Yet man's ingenuity is great, and he can make astounding progress once he sets his mind to solving a problem. There is no doubt that something can be done to improve the "fit" between spoken and written English. In this, as in other problems, we need not despair if the solution does not occur to us all at once. Let's keep on trying!

Chapter 3

Problems of Semantics

MARIO PEI

THE LANGUAGE OF DIPLOMACY

Diplomacy, the exchange of official messages and points of view between two sovereign governments, is a matter of ancient historical record. Hieroglyphic carvings in the tombs of the Pharaohs show ambassadors coming to the Egyptian court from distant lands, accompanied by interpreters. Interpreters were presumably not needed for envoys sent by one Greek city-state to another, since the language differences were at the most dialectal; but they came into play when the Greeks had to deal with the Persian empires of Darius and Artaxerxes. A *hermeneus,* or interpreter (the word comes from the name of Hermes, or Mercury, god of trade and communications and messenger of the gods), is mentioned by such writers as Xenophon and Herodotus. The Romans, in their dealings with multilingual races, made use of *legati,* appointed officials (note, however, that *legatus* could also be used in a military sense, a second in command; the root word is *lego,* to select or appoint; our *delegate* and *delegation* come from the same root).

59

Other names for envoys or ambassadors that appeared at the time of the fall of the Roman Empire, if not before, were *nuntius,* one who announces; *mandatarius,* one who transmits orders or messages; *agens,* the forerunner of our *agent; commissarius,* one to whom something is committed or entrusted (our *commissar* and *commissary*); *orator,* speaker, one who speaks a message; even *bajulatus,* "burden carrier," later "deputy," ultimately "bailiff" (the burden in this case was a semantic one). *Ambactus,* from which our *embassy* and *ambassador* are derived, was also used in imperial and late Latin. The word has a curious history. Derived originally from Celtic (in Gaulish it meant a servant), it was taken over both by the Romans and the Germanic invaders (Gothic, for example, has *andbahti* from this source). The original servant or vassal, sent on a confidential mission by his master or overlord, eventually turned into an ambassador, endowed with the attributes of inviolability, immunity, even extraterritoriality for his official residence, with the right of giving asylum to those who sought it. But these attributes were sometimes more imaginary than real. Italian has a saying *Ambasciator non porta pena,* "An ambassador carries no penalty"; but Italian also has a noun derived from the same source, *ambascia,* which means shortness of breath, anguish, distress. History and legend are both full of accounts in which the ambassador or envoy, bearing a message unpleasant to its recipient, was killed on the spot. One is forced to wonder whether the circuitous form of double talk known as diplomatic language did not originate in this connection. A harsh message could be softened and rendered more palatable by a judicious use of words, and this, too, is exemplified in both history and legend.

There are other fascinating angles to the history of diplomacy: the medieval complaint, for instance, that accredited diplomatic representatives were often *exploratores magis quam oratores,* spies rather than ambassadors, a complaint that is frequently voiced today, when diplomatic immunity, extraterritoriality, and the diplomatic pouch offer plentiful opportunities to diplomatic representatives, particularly military, naval, commercial, and scientific attachés, to pry into the secret affairs of the host nation.

The words *diplomacy* and *diplomatic* themselves come from *diploma,* which in origin is any sort of official document. Literally, the word means folded over, and arose from the ancient practice of inscribing official messages and records on two sheets of metal that were then shut together. The science of *diplomatics* technically means the study of ancient and medieval documents of any description. Since government agencies, especially those that deal with foreign relations and treaties, are particularly concerned with official documents, *diplomacy* and *diplomatic* came to be attached to such relations. The use of *diplomatic* in the sense of cautious in action and in speech is almost proverbial, and goes back to the need for such caution on the part of envoys at a time when heads of state were even touchier than they are today.

Other interesting terms connected with diplomacy are the eighteenth-century Viennese use of *diplomatic corps (corps diplomatique)* to betoken the sum total of all foreign envoys in a capital city, and the distinctions of rank in the diplomatic corps (envoy, minister, minister plenipotentiary, ambassador, depending on the importance of the two nations concerned and the desire to show each other honor); and the continued use of *nuntius,* in the form *nuncio,* to designate the Papal envoy to a nation or court (he often functions as the dean of the diplomatic corps, regardless of seniority). Of interest also is the use of a universal diplomatic language, officially used at all diplomatic gatherings. In the seventeenth and eighteenth centuries, when the international prestige of France was at its height, this distinction fell to the French language. The official texts of treaties between nations neither of which had French as its national language were nevertheless drawn up in French. The Congress of Vienna, which settled the fate of Europe after Napoleon's downfall, carried on all its proceedings in the language of the defeated nation. It was only after the First World War that English was made co-official with French at the Versailles Conference. Today, though there are five official languages at the United Nations, French and English continue to be the favorites among delegates of countries to which none of the five languages is native.

The French language is well fitted to be the language of diplomacy because of its rather regular syntax, which does not lend itself to misunderstandings, and its well-developed vocabulary, capable of conveying the most delicate shades of meaning. One can be perhaps more precise and less offensive in French than in any other tongue. Languages of equal politeness, such as Spanish and Italian, are prolix, verbose, and overelastic. Languages of equal precision, such as English, German, and Russian, are often blunt and overdirect. Bluntness coupled with precision does not hurt at all in commercial or scientific matters, but it can be dangerous in international relations. Prolixity and elasticity coupled with courtesy lend themselves well to literature and poetry, but can confuse diplomatic meanings that need to be precise and unmistakable. For these reasons, the French text still is often considered final when treaties are drawn up in two or more languages, and questions of interpretation arise.

The diplomatic language as we know it today arose largely in the seventeenth and eighteenth centuries, when politeness was more in vogue than it is now. Saber-rattling was muted, and no one dreamed of pounding the table with his shoe. Members of the diplomatic corps were usually aristocrats, both well educated and well bred. Morally, they were probably no better than the diplomats of today, but they believed in conducting their business more gracefully. A personal dispute between people of their class might be settled by a duel with rapiers or pistols, more deadly but less messy than a fistfight. Also, the danger of affairs reaching a breaking point was greater then than now. With the atom bomb and intercontinental ballistic missiles as deterrents, we and our opponents can afford rougher speech. Much of what is said today at international gatherings would inevitably have led to war in those days, when wars were far less destructive and were carried on with mercenary troops.

For all these reasons, the diplomatic language evolved in those past centuries and still generally used today strikes us as an exaggerated form of double talk, very much at variance with the blunt language of threat occasionally indulged in by the politicians and diplomats, but far more by military leaders. The elements involved in the language of diplomacy are fear of war, which is very real, coupled with a desire for an out, an escape hatch, a face-saving device. The language of the ultimatum is invariably a last resort, and the next step is war itself.

When a diplomatic note says that "our government views with grave concern" certain developments that are occurring in certain areas, the meaning may easily be "Get the hell out, or else!" When we speak about "the friendly relations that have always existed between our two nations," we may in reality be sounding a sharp warning. "We shall reluctantly be compelled to take steps to safeguard American interests" may foreshadow a landing of troops who may already be loaded on transports. "Indissolubly bound by ties of eternal friendship" may mean "Too bad you don't see things our way any longer; be careful!" One lovely sample of modern diplomatic language was President Johnson's offer of "unconditional negotiations" to Communist China and North Vietnam. It probably didn't fool anybody, but it sounded much better than Roosevelt's demand for "unconditional surrender" hurled at Germany, Japan, and Italy during World War II.

An altogether different aspect of the diplomatic language was brought out by Edmund Glenn, Chief of the Interpretation Branch of the State Department, at a conference on general semantics held in 1954. His concern is with the semantic difficulty of communication between people of different cultural background.

We are creatures of habit, and habit extends not only to language, but also to lines of thought. Translation and interpretation consist of far more than the rendering of words, phrases, and sentences. How do you render a person's thought, which is based upon his life experience, quite different from your own?

We think the Russian is a hypocrite when he speaks of Communist governments as "People's Democracies." How can any form of government be a democracy where people don't have a voting choice between at least two parties or candidates? But the Russian has been trained from childhood to think of democracy as a system in which the government is *for* the people, not necessarily, or at all, *by* the people. A family, says he, is no less a family because the father acts in what he honestly conceives to be the best interests of all members, even if he doesn't poll them to find out whether they would rather spend the vacation in the mountains or at the seashore. He, and even the others, may think the idea of polling everybody and following the poll is silly, and in any event not conducive to the best possible results. In his view, we are the hypocrites, with our insistence on a procedure he considers basically absurd, simply because all his background and training point that way.

Dr. Glenn offers two striking examples of semantic difference due to background. If you say "yes" or "no" to an Arab, he may easily interpret your "yes" as "no" and your "no" as "yes." To make it clear to him that you really mean yes or no, you must be emphatic. This is why we hear the Arab say *"La, la, la, la, la!"* at least a dozen times, shaking his head and clucking his tongue against his teeth at the same time. He may sound exaggerated to us, but all he means is "No."

Colonialism as an issue, says Dr. Glenn, found Americans solidly ranged against it. "Colonialism" made no such impression on Europeans, who were accustomed to having colonies. The word, however, reminded us of our old status as "colonies" of Great Britain, and of our Revolutionary War whereby we got rid of our colonial status. It made no difference to most Americans that conditions were vastly different in present-day Kenya, Ghana, Rhodesia, or Algeria from what they had been in the American Colonies of 1776. The world picture may well have been changed by virtue of this semantic outlook.

To emphasize his point, Dr. Glenn goes on to describe a single UN session on a minor procedural matter. Only English, French, and Russian were involved. But the differences in ideology and modes of expression were profound. There was the Soviet representative labeling certain Western stands as *nepravilnoe*, "incorrect." By this he meant not deliberately false, but based on what were to him the wrong premises. When the American delegate spoke of his country's economy as an "expanding economy," the Soviet delegate again took exception. *Expanding*, which in English could mean by reason of outside factors, has to be translated into Russian by a reflexive verb, *self-expanding*. But by definition a capitalistic economy must be a contracting one to a Communistic mind, since that is part of the teaching of Marx, Engels, and Lenin. Hence there was, to the Soviet delegate, an inherent contradiction in the American phrase.

Again, French *déduire*, whose etymological and normal translation would be English *deduce*, came out properly as *assume* in the context under consideration. This was not a scientific deduction, but rather an assumption based on the facts presented. The Russian translation, *zaklyuchat'*, on the other hand, literally meant *to conclude*. French *avis*, normally *opinion*, was in the context presented rather an assertion, or strong affirmation. French *préjuger* lent itself to two possible interpretations, *prejudice* and *prejudge*, and the translator's choice lay between the two, which do not at all carry the same meaning in English.

It is sometimes asserted that an international language

would not work well because it would force all modes of expression into the same mold, which in turn would be reflected on the mentalities of the speakers. This is perfectly true, but it is forgotten that a common language, once achieved, would tend at first to operate on a largely material plane, and pass on only slowly, and in the course of decades, to cover situations such as those described by Dr. Glenn, with plenty of possibilities of gradual semantic adjustment along the way. At any rate, anything that may be said of an international language in this connection applies in equal measure to the many languages the diplomats are forced to use today, in cleverly translated forms. Complete semantic understanding does not at all exclude the possibility of psychological and cultural discord, and it is likely that the latter can never be completely eliminated.

THE CHANGING MEANINGS OF WORDS

It is a commonplace that words tend to assume different meanings from the ones they originally had. While most Latin words survive in the Romance languages, less than half retain the Latin meanings. A verb like Latin *mittere,* to send, appears today in French *mettre,* Spanish *meter,* Italian *mettere,* but with the meaning of to put. *Focus,* which in Latin meant hearth or fireplace, has become French *feu,* Spanish *fuego,* Italian *fuoco*; but these all mean fire, not fireplace.

Occasionally there are reversals and near-reversals of meaning. Latin *nescius,* an adjective formed from *ne scio,* "I do not know," meant silly, ignorant. It retains the former meaning in French *niais,* but as it moves from French to English the word becomes *nice,* which at first still meant silly. In the language of medieval philosophy, a *nice distinction* was a silly, hairsplitting distinction; but this in turn came to be regarded as a precise, fine distinction. Ultimately, *nice* ceased to mean silly and became synonymous with *fine,* to the point where today we can speak flatteringly of

in words like *occasion* and *opportunity* (the best translation for French *occasion* is *chance,* and the best translation for French *opportunité* is *fitness, appropriateness*).

Lewd in Chaucer's day meant unlearned, ignorant; today it means licentious; *doom* changed its meaning from judgment (but we still *deem,* or judge, it best to do something) to condemnation, or even destruction; *imbecile,* once feeble-bodied, is now feeble-minded; *libertine,* once a free thinker, is now a rake; *officious* has gone from serviceable to meddlesome; *wiseacre* from wise person to smart aleck, with overtones of simpleton; *fond* from foolish to affectionate. *Marshal,* originally a horse-groom, and *constable,* originally a stable supervisor, have turned into police officers, or even high-ranking military officials (*Marshal Pétain* and *Great Constable of France*). *Quaker, Methodist, Whig, Tory,* were all originally terms of derision, appropriated by those at whom they were aimed and worn as badges of honor. *Cavalier,* more or less equivalent to *knight,* and applied to the followers of Charles I, was subverted by Cromwell's Puritans till it acquired the derogatory meaning that appears today in *cavalier treatment.* Something of a similar nature appears in *surly,* originally *sirly,* "like a sir or aristocrat." Half a century ago, *to raise* was used only in connection with cattle, and *to rear* was the proper term for children; today, we don't hesitate to "raise" a child. *Phonography* was originally a synonym for shorthand or stenography. An *undertaker* was one who undertook anything.

The King James Bible offers some startling examples of semantic change. There *admire* and *admiration* are used in the sense of to wonder at and astonishment; *base* simply means lowly, and has no bad moral connotation; but *naughty* means deeply evil. *High-minded* is proud, haughty. *Prevent* is not hinder, but precede or go before, while *even* is often used in the sense of namely. In the same period, *to coffee-house* meant to cheat at cards, and Bancroft could write of "the finest and most absolute of monarchies."

A very recent semantic change has struck the verb *to process*. If a firm that owes you money tells you your check is being "processed," it means you will have to wait at least a month for it.

One special ramification of semantic change is the one involved in linguistic taboos. In some Romance countries, such words as *Jew, Jewish, Hebrew,* are generally restricted, for no particular reason, to special uses, and the term normally used to refer to an individual is *Israelite* (not to be confused with *Israeli*). This is on a par with our habit, now in process of disappearing, of using *colored* in connection with a Negro.

Linguistic taboos, particularly when connected with races or religions, know no rhyme or reason. In *apartheid*-minded South Africa, *colored* is reserved for East Indians or half-breeds, and the native black Africans, while they may be described as Blacks, are more often referred to as *natives*. This leads to such illogical formations as *foreign native,* applied to a black African who comes from beyond the South African borders. In New Zealand, the term *native,* which seems reasonable and inoffensive enough as applied to the aboriginal Maori, is resented by them, no doubt because of connotations with which it has been invested in the past. Something similar has happened to our word *Asiatic,* in recent times generally replaced by *Asian.* It seems that Asiatics, or Asians, resent *Asiatic,* not because of anything intrinsic, but because it reminds them of the evil days of colonialism. *Asian,* presumably, fits in well with both neocolonialism and national liberation movements (note that it's always *Afro-Asian,* never *Afro-Asiatic*).

The field of linguistic taboos lends itself to other considerations. Modern literature, so-called, has made us familiar with the printed version of many of the traditional four-letter words that once appeared in writing only in unofficial inscriptions of the graffiti type. Prudishness survives residually, however, even in *Webster's Third,* which refuses to divulge or define a few words on the ground that they might contaminate schoolchildren who probably hear them every day. A writer recently drew notice by his use of the highly euphemistic *pudendum.*

This type of linguistic taboo has vast ramifications. *Heirconditioned* for *pregnant,* and *derrière* for something else come to mind. What is euphemistically known as a *rest room* or *powder room* in America often disguises itself as a *cloak room* in Britain, to the discomfiture of American tourists, who can't find what they are looking for no matter how hard they look. In this particular connection, it is downright humorous to observe what euphemisms have been created in most civilized languages to denote what should be denoted in simple terms. Italian and Spanish use "retreat," and German, that most direct of Western languages, calls it *Abort* ("awayplace"); French favors an English term, *water closet,* which the English apparently put into circulation but later gave up; but French further disguises it by pluralizing and abbreviating it (*les W.C.*); Russian uses an *ubornaya,* which has to do with adornment, like our *toilet* (from French *toilette,* small piece of cloth). Even Melanesian pidgin has devised a suitable euphemism, *house peck-peck.*

Taboos and euphemisms abound in the various occupations and professions. *Undertaker* was once used etymologically in the sense of one who undertakes (modern *entrepreneur*); becoming specialized in the sense of one who undertakes a funeral operation (or, perhaps, even more literally, one who takes you underground), it seemed too blunt, and *mortician* was suggested as a replacement. This goes along with *beautician* for a beauty-parlor operator, even *linguistician* for linguist (on the ground that *linguist* is often used in the sense of *polyglot*). *Saloon* has gone on to *bar,* and that in turn to *cocktail lounge.* A clerk has become a *junior executive,* and an old man a *senior citizen.* A maid has turned into a *domestic worker,* a housewife into a *homemaker,* a porter into a *redcap,* a laborer into a *wage earner.* An elegant *whoreson* has been suggested as a replacement for a fighting word, usually summarized in print as *S.O.B.*

And what of the feminine vocabulary, made up of hyperboles and diminutives (*heavenly, divine, darling, dolly,* on the one hand; *nightie, hanky, panties, scanties, undies, nappies,* on the other, along with names of colors that only women can distinguish, such as *beige, mauve, taupe*)? It surely was not a woman who first coined *togetherness,* but it is likely that a woman began to use it to describe that rather repulsive set of modern American customs whereby a father is supposed to be a pal and chum to his son, and a candidate for office cannot afford to appear in public without at least his wife (preferably pregnant; much better if the children are in the picture, too), under penalty of flunking out with the voters. Such euphemisms as the American *powder room* and *molest,* the British *cloak room* and *interfere with,* also seem due to feminine influence. It may be added that "molesting" and "interfering with" appear in the most extraordinary circumstances, where the victim of a sexual assault is also the victim of murder. Is this not carrying euphemism too far?

The trouble with taboo words and their replacements is that the replacement quickly tends to develop its own taboo, whereupon it, too, has to be replaced. Objections to taboos and euphemisms are of no avail whatsoever. Both constitute a definite part of usage, and both will continue, presumably, as long as language (any language) exists.

With the possible exception of taboos, most of the changes described above may be called accidental rather than deliberate. There is another type of semantic change in which the process is wanted and forced, for a special purpose. Either an existing word is used in a new connotation that contradicts the older, or it is invested with semantic charges and associated with other words so as to produce a certain effect. It is this part of semantic change that bears watching.

Here come those words which Theodore Roosevelt once

called *weasel words*—forms that sneak into the vocabulary and play havoc with the field of semantics, like a weasel in a hencoop. Special interests wanting to bring about certain changes in popular outlook, wanting to sell products or ideas, having any kind of an ax to grind—they know the power of words, slogans, catch phrases, and proceed deliberately to act upon this knowledge. New coinages are devised and put into circulation. These may be brand-new words or combinations of old words. Existing words that had for centuries led a normal existence and fulfilled their honest semantic function are invested with new overtones, designed either to enhance the word and what it stands for, or to debase it and make it and what it symbolizes an object of scorn, ridicule, or dislike. New semantic contents are attached to old words in the same fashion that one attaches a time bomb to a clock for booby-trapping purposes. This is often done by surrounding the old, time-honored words with modifiers of an enhancing or debasing nature, and using the combination over and over again, until the central word is so thoroughly imbued with the ennobling or disparaging connotation desired that the modifiers can be removed, and the effect will be the same.

We have already seen how this process of semantic denaturation is carried on by commercial advertising for the purpose of selling a product. We have yet to see how it is conducted on the political front, both domestic and international, for the purpose of selling ideas, principles, movements, forms of government.

The essence of the semantic war is propaganda, and the essence of propaganda is the use and misuse of words. The results, as we have already seen, are far-reaching. Invest a word like *colonialism* with a disreputable halo by reminding Americans that they once suffered from colonial status, and colonial empires begin to topple. Neutralize words like *liberty* and *democracy* by appropriating them and applying them to systems that are basically slavery and absolutism, and you have deprived your opponents of their best and most legitimate

weapons. Bring *profits* into disrepute by constantly surrounding the word with adjectives like *bloated, extortionate, excessive,* and you begin to demolish the system of private
enterprise. Such is the power of words.

THE LANGUAGE OF PROPAGANDA

The term *propaganda* is of religious origin. In 1622, the
Roman Catholic Church created a commission of cardinals
charged with supervising the activities of Catholic missions.
This commission was called *Congregatio de Propaganda Fide,*
Congregation for the Propagation of the Faith, or even more
literally, "concerning the faith to be spread." *Propaganda*
itself is a gerundive form of the verb *propago,* to spread or
propagate, and modifies and agrees with *fide,* the ablative
form of *fides,* faith, required by the preposition *de. Propago*
itself is a compound of *pro,* forth, and *pango,* to fix, establish
solidly.

The first appearance of *propaganda* in English was in 1718,
but in a purely religious sense. It was not until 1842 that it was
extended to cover any concerted movement for the spreading
of any and all ideas. *Propagandism,* in a religious sense, first
appears in 1818, and *propagandist,* in the sense of missionary,
in 1833, going on to cover any spreader of any ideas in 1856.
Propagandize, in both meanings, the religious and the general, appears in 1844.

Much older words coming from the same root are *propagate* and *propagation,* which go back to 1600 and 1588, respectively. Ideas were propagated before they were propagan-
dized.

The first truly sinister connotation in connection with
propaganda seems to have arisen at the time of the First World
War, when a good deal was made of pro-German propaganda.
Ever since that time an unpleasant aura has been attached, in
America, to *propaganda* and its vehicle, the language of
propaganda.

It goes without saying that propaganda can be of many different kinds. The language of commercial advertising is superlatively a form of propaganda, designed to sell the idea of and desirability of the product the sponsor wants to sell. Nevertheless, such is the force of habit that one seldom hears *commercial* and *propaganda* in the same breath. In the American popular mind, propaganda is indissolubly linked with political activities, both domestic and international.

In European countries and languages, the word *propaganda* is not invested with the unsavory connotations it arouses in the American mind. Many European countries have a Minister of Propaganda, which in America would be unthinkable, though we might well consider a Secretary of Public Relations, which would in essence amount to the same thing. Goebbels was Hitler's Propaganda Minister, and it was he who took care to spread the network of lies, rumors, and false accusations for which the Nazi regime made itself famous, or infamous, throughout the world. But long before Hitler, another movement had developed propaganda (in the American, not the European sense) into a fine art.

The Communist regime, immediately after its takeover in what used to be the Russian Empire, went to work to build not merely an idea-spreading machine, but a brand-new form of language (the so-called Aesopian language, a double talk the full meaning of which is known only to its initiates), for which the guidelines had been set by the chief Communist apostles, Marx, Engels, and Lenin, in their writings, and the structure and purpose of which are plain to anyone who cares to investigate those writings. Basing itself upon what is variously known as dialectical materialism or historical determinism, the Communist gospel proclaims that all existing regimes and social structures are doomed without reprieve, by reason of their inherent weaknesses and injustices, and are to be replaced by a universal Communistic state in which there will be no social classes or economic differences, but all people will be on a basis of absolute equality ("From everyone according to his ability, to everyone according to his need" is the formula for this ideal state). For an unspecified period of time, surpervision over this new type of social-economic-political structure and all its citizens (ideally, the entire population of the world) will be exercised by the Communist Party, the strong right arm of the proletarian class, the only one that will survive. Eventually, when all men have learned to be brothers and live in perfect harmony in the classless society, the Communist state will wither and pass away, because there will be no further need for government of any kind. The Communist mind brushes aside the logical inconsistency between its tenets and the fact that human nature, with its inherent selfishness and preference for those near and dear to the individual rather than for mankind at large, cannot be abolished or changed. All men will be brothers under the watchful eye of Big Brother—or else! And this will go on until they have learned to be brothers without that watchful eye—a day that will never dawn.

The Communist theory also brushes aside as invalid any argument that man's lot may be improved under the existing systems. These systems are thoroughly rotten and must be overthrown, by violence if need be. Any seeming improvement under the present systems must be opposed as retarding the day of the big change. To fulfill this goal, true Communists will do their best to spread discord where there is harmony, class war where there is class cooperation, poverty and hunger where there is abundance. We must all advance as one, or not at all.

Granted these ideological premises, which the Communist accepts as articles of faith, it is not surprising that he has developed not merely his own mentality, but his own type of language. Since everything that leads to Communism is good, and everything that opposes or retards Communism bad, war is not *per se* reprehensible. However aggressive and bloody its features, war is a "national liberation movement," a "defensive war," a "peace-loving war" if initiated by the Communists. It is a "capitalistic," "imperialistic," "colonialistic," "aggressive" war if carried on by a non-Communist regime, even in self-defense. When the Soviets invaded Poland and Finland in the early days of World War II, they were carrying on a purely defensive war, as was their ally Hitler in his invasion of Poland, Denmark, Norway, Holland, and Belgium. But when Hitler turned on them and attacked Russia, he became a monster of aggression.

The Aesopian language of Communism is the linguistic manifestation of a mental blank wall as hard to penetrate as any Berlin has to offer. But in addition, it is a fighting tool, something Communism uses for purposes of deception, so that the non-Communist countries will let down their guard, or with the aim of impressing those same non-Communist countries with the basic idea that they and their systems are a thing of the past, and that they may as well give way gracefully and allow themselves to be taken over.

Accordingly, we get, for consumption in the Communist countries and abroad, such stock phrases as *monolithic,* to describe the structure of Communism and of the Communist establishment; *solidarity* and *fraternal cooperation,* euphemisms for Soviet economic exploitation of satellite nations; *people's,* to describe whatever is run by the Communist bosses, as in *People's Democracy* and *People's Democratic Republic; toilers,* a stronger term that replaces an older *workers,* whose content has been diluted now that millionaires like Rockefeller or Kennedy put in ten and twelve hours a day at their working desks (*toiler,* in addition, conveys the connotation of manual labor, performed with the sweat of one's brow).

For the countries that still labor under the delusion that the old system can be saved, there is a wide range of terms. At the very least they are described as "reactionary" and "decadent," but if they show any sign of fighting back and trying to contain Communism they become "monopolistic," "militaristic," "imperialistic," "chauvinistic," "colonialistic" or "neocolonialistic," "warmongers." Their more conservative elements become "extreme rightists" and "fascists." If, on the other hand, they display a willingness to go along with the Communist master plan in its long-range objectives, the boon of "peaceful coexistence" is held out to them to lull them to sleep. If they step ouside their own boundaries to defend their interests, "Yankee go home!" makes a perfect slogan.

Since, however, the Communist world is far from being as monolithic as it would like its opponents to believe (here human nature, with its eternal basic selfishness and greed for power, comes into play), there has developed over the years an entire vocabulary of vituperation that the comrades use among themselves: *doctrinaire, bourgeois reformists, dogmatism, sectarianism, capitulationism, revisionism, deviationism, cult of personality. Irresponsible* and *sabotage* are two favorite terms in this division.

Since the capitalistic regimes were not born yesterday, and are themselves aware of a few propaganda tricks, they have developed an anti-Communist vocabulary of their own. Starting with Churchill's "Iron Curtain" (not original with him, by the way [1]), and going on to "Bamboo Curtain," we have turned "Berlin Wall" into a symbol of what might be styled the neoisolationism of the twentieth century into which the Communists have plunged their citizenry. *Satellites* is a term universally applied to states under the domination of the Communist Big Two; in applying it, we tend to forget that the term could with almost equal justification be applied to many of the nations under our protective wing, or, better yet, "atomic umbrella." *Peacenik* and *Vietnik* are terms applied rather indiscriminately to all who do not approve of our actions in Vietnam. In defense of our own way of life, we have

[1] First used, apparently, by Joseph Paul Goebbels, Nazi Propaganda Minister, on February 23, 1945. Attempting to justify the Nazi invasion of the Soviet Union, he said: "If the German people lay down their arms, the whole of eastern and southern Europe, together with the Reich, will come under Russian occupation. Behind an iron curtain, mass butcheries of people would begin."

coined such terms as *free enterprise system* and *people's capitalism* to replace the older *rugged individualism*.

Reds, pinkos, fellow-travelers, are all terms devised not only to describe, but also to expose domestic members of the Communist conspiracy, but occasionally used rather loosely. Their recipients reply with a well-chosen word-stock: *red-baiting, book-burning, witch-hunting, McCarthyism, extremism, Far Right, Radical Right, John Birchers, lunatic fringe. Police brutality* is a slogan that was coined and used by the pro-Communists long before it was appropriated by civil rights movements.

On the national political front, there is a whole world of semantic uses that distinguish our major currents. The conservative wing marks itself by the frequent use of such terms as *spiraling inflation, creeping socialism, abundant life, American way of life, anti-American activities.* The "liberal" element (note that *liberal* is a misnomer in this context, since historically and etymologically it should betoken opposition to government controls and a tendency to favor individual freedom and initiative) revels in such Presidential slogans as New Deal, Fair Deal, New Frontier, Great Society, Alliance for Progress, War on Poverty. They oppose "special interests." Then there are such euphemistic, semiofficial coinages as *senior citizen* for oldster and *dis-saver* or *negative saver* for people who are perennially in debt.

But liberal semantic creations have the undoubted merit of being generally inoffensive, not in the sense that they are ineffective, but only that they are not insulting. There is a lulling quality to such formations as *consensus* and *mainstream*, with their appeal to what is hoped will be a majority. One of the greatest propaganda triumphs in history was the attaching of the label *moderates* to the opponents of Barry Goldwater and his conservatives in the 1964 campaign. This was semantically on a par with the coinage, for propaganda purposes, of the earlier label *temperance movements* for teetotalers and prohibitionists (*temperance,* in its historical acceptance, means reasonable use of a nonharmful variety, not total abstention enforced by unenforceable laws). Some voters found it easy to choose between the "moderation" seemingly advocated by Kennedy-Johnson Democrats and Rockefeller-Lodge Republicans and the "extremism" (even though qualified by "in defense of liberty") propounded by Goldwater and his conservatives.

Another area in which sloganeering has gained the upper hand over reason is the field of taxation. Here "the ability to pay" and "fairest form of taxation" have cast a halo over the steeply graduated income tax, which an earlier and franker generation had more brutally sloganized as "soak the rich" legislation. On the other hand, a member of the capitalistic set was once heard to remark that he was being "taxed out of existence as a class."

Other slogan words are dispensed in connection with foreign-aid programs. Here the recipient nations have long been described as *have-not, underdeveloped, emergent* (or *emerging;* Eleanor Roosevelt's "fledgeling nations" unfortunately did not take hold). The words are clearly calculated to arouse sympathy and imbue us with a sense that we are somehow responsible for the plight of countries like warring India and Pakistan, sword-waving Nasser's Egypt, and Nkrumah's Ghana. *Global commitments* is another phrase frequently used. When the recipients of our economic foreign aid go over to the enemy, they are mildly described as *neutralistic, non-committed, unaligned.* One of the most astounding and ingenious coinages was Secretary of Agriculture Orville Freeman's "concessional exports" to describe what the other side, using a loaded, journalistic expression, calls a *giveaway* program, further claiming that it has emptied our wheat and corn bins to the danger level. For the program of cooperation and "understanding" with an enemy that means to bury us, we have such expressions as *collective security, tension reduction, surrender of sovereignty.*

The civil rights movement has evolved a large and flourishing vocabulary, on both sides of the fence. Here we have such terms as *White Supremacy; Never!; white, Anglo-Saxon, Protestant* (WASP); *blockbusting; backlash* (and *frontlash*) on one side; on the other, *racist* and *racism* (words so recently coined that they do not appear in the 1930 *Oxford Dictionary*); *Black Muslim* and *Black Power; Freedom Riders; sit-in, kneel-in, teach-in* (but *sit-in*, used in connection with strikes, goes back to labor practices of the 1930's); *fearmongers, hatemongers, hate groups,* even *hatenanny*, used to describe a gathering of Lincoln Rockwell's neo-Nazis. Integration and segregation are surrounded with emotion-arousing words (*racial, cultural*), or euphemized into *racial imbalance.* The statement *We got the white man on the run* is, in its own way, a classic. While terms of insult abound (*nigger, jigaboo, whitey, ofay*), one of the most picturesque creations, designed to perpetuate dissension in the face of expanding integration and equality, is *tokenism.* In the view of some of the more extreme civil rights leaders, any Negro who makes a success of himself and is accepted on his own merits becomes a mere "token" of integration, and may be further qualified with such ironic expressions as *Uncle Tom, Aunt Thomasina, Doctor Thomas.* It is conveniently forgotten (1) that all white people are far from making the grade; (2) that as the Negroes achieve their rightful place in American society, the number of "tokens" tends to outstrip that of nontokens.

One interesting verb, again of such recent coinage that it does not appear in the 1930 *Oxford,* is *ghettoize.* It is used (and misused) by left-wing writers and reviewers who take umbrage at any separate mention of Jews or Negroes, even if the mention is highly favorable.

Under the circumstances, it may be of interest to see what the courts consider libelous in the matter of name-calling, to the point of awarding damages.

In the late 1800's it was libel to call a person a "Mormon." This was because the practice of polygamy was considered a national threat. At the turn of the century it was libelous to call a person an "anarchist," and after the Russian Revolution even "socialist" came under the court's ban.

In the South, as late as the 1930's, it was libel to call a white man "colored," and in the 1950's, during the McCarthy era, it became libelous to describe someone in print as a "Communist sympathizer." In 1965 an Ohio court declared it libelous to call a Negro an "Uncle Tom," but this was reversed by the Supreme Court of that state.

In 1966 the Court of Appeals of the District of Columbia declared it libelous to call a man a "bigot."

It would therefore appear that there are definite legal limits to the use of the language of political and racial propaganda, at least as applied to specific individuals.

The language of political propaganda has at least two further ramifications of a semipolitical nature, to the extent that their adepts indulge frequently in activities of a political nature. One is education, particularly of the sociological variety; the other is labor.

The language of education has already been referred to in Chapter I. Its gobbledygook has been described, but the following passage will refresh the reader's memory: "The common denominator of those subcultures whose specializing influences are largely alien to the demands of middle class norms is poverty." The best translation here seems to be, "Those people who aren't in the middle class are usually poor."

New-school "educationists" [2] have evolved a vocabulary and a set of semantics designed to make people think that if anything is wrong, it is largely their own fault. To foster this state of mind, the socio-educational reformers have devised a vocabulary that includes the old *underprivileged* and the more recent (*socially*) *disadvantaged*; also *insecure, malad-*

[2] *Educationist* as opposed to *educator* is a loaded word, coined by the opponents of so-called progressive education to describe its professional advocates in the schools.

justed, frustrated, repressed, culturally deprived, culturally different (the last is purely a euphemism). It will be noted that *culture* and *culturally* are used in accordance with the new anthropological definition rather than the older, in which *culture* betokened something intellectually superior. The current anthropological definition of *culture* is any set of habits, customs, and thoughtways that may characterize a social group, high or low, literate or illiterate, civilized or savage.

More specific creations for the field of education are such words as *mentally retarded, emotionally disturbed, unstable, abnormal*. Certain individuals may be described as "problems," posing the universal "challenge" (in the privacy of their offices, the teachers often call a "problem child" by a more direct name, a "pain in the neck"). A *dyslexic* child is one who finds it difficult to learn to read. There is "latent ability" and "untapped potential" in some cases, and "underachievers" are occasionally compensated for by "overachievers," who may also be described as "intellectually gifted" and "exceptional." There is "need imbalance" and there are "unfelt needs" on the part of students, for whom are prescribed "cultural immersion" and "vital learning experiences," fortified by "motivational research" and "corrective feedback," and leading to "enrichment." (It used to be "education for leadership," but it gradually became evident that education for followership was about as much as could be expected of the majority of students, and that in any case it was impractical to have all chiefs and no Indians).

Other choice educational terms are *motion potential, unit content, manipulative skills* (being able to do something with your hands), *teacher bias* (this is where the teacher explodes). *Effectuate* and *verbalize* are two favorite verbs. It is fashionable to speak of "language arts" or, better yet, "communications arts," rather than of English and foreign languages. For the latter, we have the "aural-oral" or, to use a fresher variant, "audio-lingual" methodology; this is the parrot method of learning languages, favored over the ancient grammatical approach, which forced people to use their brains as well as their reflexes.

One more term—the word *exciting*—may be mentioned, which stems from the language of advertising and commercialism but seems to be spreading in educational milieus. In the older language *exciting* had a stronger connotation than it seems to have today. Everything has to be "exciting." In the watered-down present-day acceptance, we find a children's encyclopedia recommending that the article on language be made "exciting" to the youthful readers. To one brought up with the older connotation, this brings up visions of children dancing and yelling with glee because they have just discovered that English is an Indo-European language.

The labor union movement has in the course of many decades evolved a special vocabulary, with terms that have acquired an aura of sanctity not only to union members, but also to politicians who court the labor vote. For example, we often hear such hallowed and mouth-filling terms as *negotiations* and *collective bargaining*. To the innocent bystander, these refer to the period during which the gun is pointed at his head, but doesn't quite go off. All kinds of "benefits" ("fringe" and otherwise) come into play, as does a very real "cost of living" factor. Next comes a "strike vote," followed by the setting of a "strike deadline," which is the most deadly thing in the whole procedure, since it is the full equivalent of the good old ultimatum in international relations. "Give us what we want by a certain hour on a certain day—or else" is the burden of both ultimatum and strike deadline. After that it is war, and the bombs fall where they may, which in the case of the strike is usually on the head of the hapless consumer. Now comes the sacred "picket line," which no man or woman may cross under penalty, at the very least, of being called a "scab," "fink," "rat," or worse. *Solidarity* is a term occasionally used to proclaim that members of one union will not cross another union's picket line, but since the term has Communist overtones, it is more often avoided. *Security* is sometimes used, but since it is an all-purpose term, it is generally preceded by *job*.

It is interesting to watch the working of the other process of semantic change, that of investing an innocent word with explosive connotations by constantly surrounding it with appropriate modifiers. In one union periodical, the word *profits* never stands alone. Profits are invariably "fat," "bloated," "extortionate"; at the very least, "unreasonable" or "excessive." One newspaper writer contended that Vice President Humphrey, addressing the United Auto Workers, had implied by his treatment that *profits* is a dirty word. After being exposed to this sort of brainwashing for a year or so, any union member is guaranteed to see red when the word *profits* is mentioned, even if all adjectives are removed and the profits are legitimate.

Management publications have their own semantic weapon arsenal, however: *high wages, excellent working conditions, generous fringe benefits, American living standards,* and, of course, *American free enterprise,* coupled with snide references to the unions' *unreasonable demands, demagogic leadership, gouging practices, questionable political affiliations.*

There is occasional humor in the situation. One cartoon character says to another: "He's a true capitalist. Never uses the word 'social' in the same breath with 'revolution' or 'justice' "!

Within and without the military establishment, there is a rather frequent use of words that seem designed to foster certain states of mind and are, to that extent, of a propaganda nature. Hawks and doves vie in linguistic creation and semantic adaptation. One segment of the military language, without being forthrightly propagandistic, seems designed to underplay certain obvious facts of modern military affairs and to familiarize us with what may turn out to be the inevitable, so that we may face it without flinching and also, perhaps, without protesting.

There is, to begin with, the use of *defense* in connection with what used to be known as *war*. Why should a military establishment be known as the Department of Defense when its mission is to carry on offensive as well as defensive conflict? Under modern as well as older conditions, *defense* is a rank euphemism.

Other words in the same class are *conventional* (in connection with either war or weapons; are you any less dead if you are killed by a "conventional" weapon, such as a rifle or bayonet?); *deterrence* (you don't "deter" an enemy; you blast him if he makes the first move, or even if he does not; the "atomic umbrella" is said to be a form of deterrence); *survivability* (this is your chance of living through an atomic conflict).

Top credit for inventiveness in the field of military euphemisms goes to Truman for his description of the Korean war as a "police action." Luckily, no one has yet called the Vietnam war a police action. Here the best euphemism is still Johnson's "unconditional negotiations." *Escalation* is a word so recent that it does not appear at all in the *Oxford,* and in the 1961 *Webster's* only in a commercial acceptance (to make price adjustments to compensate for certain disadvantages). In the same 1961 dictionary, *to escalate* means only to convey goods by means of a lift or escalator. *Modernization* (of weapons) is legitimate, as is Eisenhower's *infrastructure.* But the language of our generals also has such terms as *city bargaining* ("You spare New York and we'll spare Moscow"); *to take out a city* (in the sense of to obliterate it with one well-aimed ballistic missile carrying an atomic warhead); *unacceptable damage* (what we, or the others, cannot take in the way of atomic bombardment, leading, presumably, to surrender, if anyone is left to surrender or surrender to).

The advocates of "appeasement" (definitely a loaded word) on atomic-missile grounds have their own vocabulary to offer

It is so voluble and changing, so highly localized in time, that it is almost impossible to record it on any sort of permanent basis. Here perhaps more than anywhere else we see the basic correctness of the Latin saying *Verba volant,* "Words fly away."

As a single example of picturesque teen-age usage, we may take something from another language. Italian teen-agers call people over twenty-five "78-revs" (78 revolutions per minute, the speed of the old short-playing records).

For our own language, a highly interesting brochure by Eric Partridge, entitled "A Square Digs Beatnik," appeared in 1960. It has the double merit of being an evaluation from abroad (therefore more impartial and less subjective than native material would be) and of fixing the teen-age-beatnik language at the point of its zenith.

After making some observations concerning *beatnik,* defined as the language, partly slang, partly jargon, spoken by the "Beat Generation," the genial British slang expert gives the three current explanations of *beat* (beaten-down or down-trodden, beatific, and beat-worshiping, with *beat* used as a synonym for *jazz rhythm*). Partridge rejects the second interpretation, advanced by Jacques Kerouac, and favors the last.

Examples of the vocabulary of teen-age beatniks are *chick* for girl, *drop* for "drop dead" (not to be interpreted literally, but only in the mild sense of "go away," "stop bothering me"; other replacements, not mentioned by Partridge, are *D.D.T.,* short for "drop dead twice," and *turn blue*). *Cat, cool, crazy, dig, end* (or *the end,* an absolute superlative), *goof, hip, man* (as a form of direct address), *square,* and *swing* (or *swinging*) are further gems. Additional favorite terms are *something else* (almost as much of an absolute superlative as *the end*), *go* and *gone* (in teen-age parlance, the second is not the past participle of the first), *(the) most, way out, hang-up,* and *pad,* both noun and verb.

Square, traced back to jazz musicians, is said to come from steady 1-2-3-4 rhythm without variations, as exemplified by a band director's gesture in which the hand moves in the form of a square. But for this "unimaginative," "stuffy" interpretation Partridge claims concurrent influence from an earlier British *square* in the sense of fair, upright (as in *square deal*). This would make the "square" a person of conventional morals, who tries to be equitable, but does not have much in the way of fire or imagination.

Dig is explained as to understand, to agree with, to get to the bottom of things, as well as to observe, admire, and appreciate. Partridge reminds us that it was used at a much earlier period by British con men in the more literal sense of to make inquiries and contacts, to case the joint.

Hip, "in the know," with its derivatives, *hipster* and *hippie*, is traced back to an earlier *hep*, meaning shrewd, alert, possibly from a teamster's "Hep! Hep!" as a call of encouragement to his horses.

The adjective *cool* implies a "laudable detachment or moderation or poise." Partridge does not mention the more recent American contribution, in the form of a functional shift to a verb ("Cool it, man!"). *Cool* has now become a noun as well, and instead of losing their tempers hotheads who are with-it lose their "cool."

Cat was once a tramp new to the road, or an itinerant worker. *Gay cat* meant that the cat was inexperienced. But a *cool cat* may turn into "something else," becoming "hip" or "hep," and "digging" things correctly. *Way out* is rendered as "enigmatic" and "abstract," *crazy* as "fabulously interesting," *(real) gone* as "inspired by music." *Swing* and *swinging* cover the general area of having the basic feel for jazz rhythms, but then branch out into "to get the feel of," "to comprehend the truth and beauty of anything worth digging." *Pad* is either a bed or a habitation, and "Pad me!" is a cat's invitation to a chick to share his room and bed; the expression goes back to sixteenth-century English use of *pad* as a bundle of straw to lie on.

Go is treated by Partridge as a native word. But I have the feeling that it must have been at least influenced by French *à gogo,* "aplenty," "in abundance," which frequently appears in discothèque inscriptions.

Indicative of slang's tendency to change and dialectalize is that the *with it* that Partridge mentions and describes, while still current in America, tends in Britain, according to latest information, to be replaced by *in the wind,* just as the very numerous terms for money are now tending to be replaced by *bread. He's in the dough, His garden is green, He's got lettuce,* represent different time-layers of twentieth-century teenage slang. Whereas an older generation, once young, spoke of a girl's legs as her *shafts* or *gams,* a later generation describes them as her *future.* The former *wolf* may now be a *make-out artist.*

Some teen-age creations have a logical basis—*cheesecloth* for someone obvious, *upper plates* for the older generation, *wig* or *bird* for girl. Others sound like weird foreign languages, or sounds from another planet—*ub-glub, oo-pop-ada, lu-e-pa, lu-cu-pu, dil-ya-bla, low-pow, bong, oogley, bongo-bongo* (translations: strange, funny, What's the matter?, Good night, Hello, OK, good, excellent, I'm surprised). A word of caution: don't be bongo-bongo if your current teen-agers are unacquainted with these expressions; it has been estimated that the vocabulary turns over completely every four years (the normal duration of a high school course).

The question arises whether this use of a special teen-age slang constitutes an obstacle to understanding among the various generations that have to coexist, however little they may like it. The answer is an emphatic Yes. Parents are often accused of not "understanding" their children. This accusation is as often as not literal. The real question is whether it is the linguistic difference that leads to the psychological lack of understanding and sympathy, whether the psychological difference arises first, and is more or less naturally followed by a linguistic differentiation, or whether the two factors simultaneously work upon and reinforce each other. What must be kept in mind is that the process is anything but new, and that the *skiddoo* of the twenties struck the ears of people born and raised in the Victorian era as unpleasantly as today's *scram* affects those of us who are squares by reason of age. The change in teen-age language is so kaleidoscopic that any attempt to crystallize the language in print dooms the writer to obsolescence before his book is published.

As for the manifestations of the phenomenon of combined linguistic and psychological lack of understanding, they are best summarized by the episode of a grandmother who was telling her very young granddaughter that there were two words she didn't want to hear the little girl use: "One is swell, the other is lousy." "OK, Grandma," replied the little girl. "What are the two words?"

THE PROBLEM OF CULTURAL MISUNDERSTANDING

One final aspect of semantics concerns the different meanings attached to the same word by different groups, or sub-cultures. We have already seen how the word *culture* may denote two radically different, practically opposite things, depending on whether it is used by a literary specialist or by an anthropologist. We have also seen how different meanings attached to the same word may affect diplomatic and international relations.

Similar confusions may easily occur within the same language group. *Conventional* is subject to a very special meaning when employed by the military. *Security* and *benefits* mean one thing to the union leader angling for a more favorable contract, something else to the recipient of an old-age pension or annuity. *Garbage,* which has a very specific meaning to the housewife, in space talk means objects ejected from the space vehicle to float around forever; but in computer language it refers to odds and ends of information disgorged by the computer in the course of its operations, but extraneous to the purpose for which the computer is being operated.

My editor tells the story of a friend who was searching for a book on cylinder seals, and was led to the auto-mechanics section of the store.

A Washington social leader was once asked what she thought about Red China. She replied without hesitation: "It depends upon what kind of tablecloth you use." *Red* itself, which to us has overtones of violence and radicalism, is in Russian associated with the root of *beauty* and *beautiful*. It is the color of fire and warmth, while white is the color of the snowy, frozen wastes in which one can perish. In the Russian Revolution this gave the Red Guard a big psychological advantage over the White Armies of Denikin and Kolchak.

National designations are more subject to distortion than ordinary words. To us, the label *American* brings up all sorts of pleasant connotations. This is not true of British users of the language, many of whom tend to view anything "American" with reservations. In other countries, and in other connections, the connotations may be even more unfavorable. The French call a con game or swindle *vol à l'américaine,* American-style theft. *Invitation à l'américaine* is what we call a Dutch treat. *Coups de poing américains* are brass knuckles. There is also *avoir le coup d'oeil américain* (literally, "to have the American glance") for "to observe without seeming to look"; but the reference here seems to be to the American Indians. *Oncle d'Amérique* for "rich uncle" is rather flattering. The Italians speak of *un'americanata* to refer to something done flamboyantly and loudly, particularly for publicity purposes; the verb *americaneggiare* means to ape the Americans, and is definitely derogatory. In Spanish the expression *cosas de América,* things of America, refers to any wildly improbable story; but it is not the present United States or its inhabitants that are involved; the expression arose in the early days of exploration and discovery, when the men of Columbus, de Soto, and Ponce de León came back with extravagant accounts of what they had seen in the New World (Eldorado and the Seven Golden Cities of Cibola go back to the same period). Surprisingly, it is the Russians and Chinese who favor us semantically. The former call a beauty salon *amerikanka,* American woman; the latter call our country *Mei Kuo,* beautiful land.

Before we take umbrage at some of the above misuses of our national name, let us consider for an instant what we do to others. *Dutch uncle, Dutch courage,* even *Dutch treat* are not exactly calculated to flatter the Dutch. Neither do *German measles* and *German cockroach* flatter the Germans. *To welch* (or *welsh*) on an obligation can hardly please the inhabitants of Wales.

At any rate, this sort of usage is altogether international. The Italians refer to venereal disease as *the French malady,* and the French call it *English.* The Japanese call the bedbug *Nanking insect,* blaming it on the Chinese. The Slavic term for Germans meant in origin dumb, unspeaking. Even the ancient Greeks called all non-Greek speakers *barbarians* or *babblers.* And the common American expression indicating hopeless bewilderment, *It's Greek to me,* hardly flatters the Greeks or their language.

Relativity of meaning ought not to surprise anyone in these days when relativity has been established even for what we once fondly thought was a stable physical universe. Different meanings for what is ostensibly the same word-symbol constitute perhaps the main element in the semantic crisis that in turn seems to constitute the main barrier between the Communist world and our own.

Or perhaps people know only too well not only what they want and mean, but what their opponents want and mean. It is no doubt a tendency to oversimplification that leads us to reason along lines that, carried to their logical conclusion, would negate the basic causes for all conflict, not only international, but internecine as well. Yet the illusion persists that everything is reducible to semantics, that if only words didn't fail us in communicating with our fellow men all would be well. It is my own guess that all would not be well. Too many civil wars among people speaking the same language and having the same national background prove otherwise.

Yet it is a fact that words seem to fail us in the hour of our greatest need. A writer once said: "The things one loves, lives, and dies for are not completely expressible in words. . . . To write or speak is almost inevitably to lie a little." Lie to ourselves, or to others? Or both? Another, older writer put it this way: "The use of language to convey thoughts is on a par with mending a watch with a pick, or painting a miniature with a mop. Words are parvenu people compared with thoughts and actions."

Gide gave perhaps the most concrete expression to the concept of the relativity of language: "*My country* does not suggest the same landscape to peasants in Picardy and Provence, to the ploughman and the poet, to the poor and the rich. But it is a rallying-cry, and all rise to defend it, though the peasant is actually defending cultivated fields, the poet culture in general, the manufacturer industrial wealth, the shareholder his dividends."

To be even more concrete, what do *near* and *far* mean? Mars is near the Earth as compared with the nearest constellation, but very far away as compared with the moon. A man of forty is "old" if he tries to win a prizefight, but "young" if he tries to win the Presidency of the United States. Sweden and the USSR both enjoy forms of government described as "socialistic," but there is a great deal of difference between the two varieties of socialism.

It is sometimes asked whether it is possible to control meanings so that a word will convey exactly the same thing to all speakers of the language, thereby minimizing the effects of linguistic propaganda. Attempts to do this in the past have invariably failed. Both the French and the Italian academies have at various times endeavored to fix meanings, but without success. The Gillette Safety Razor people once studied the possibility of getting the language academies to declare that the name of Gillette should not be used, as it regularly is in the Latin countries, to denote any kind of safety razor, but it was pointed out to them that even if such a ruling could be obtained, it would be disregarded by the speakers, who would go right on in their evil ways.

Linguistically, the word is the symbol or, as Ferdinand de Saussure puts it, the "signifier." The object symbolized is the "signified." Ideally, there should be a definite link and a definite equivalence between the two. But no matter how material, objects are psychologically valid only in the frame of our own experience. One may try to explain a palm tree to an Eskimo, or snow to an inhabitant of the Amazonian rain forest. But how valid is the picture evoked when it is not backed up by direct experience? As a child coming from Rome, where I had never seen a snowfall, I had a mental image of snowflakes as approximately the size of a hat, an impression probably created by the Italian expression *La neve cade a larghe falde*, "The snow falls in large hat brims"; the New York reality was a disappointment to me. If this can happen with material objects, how much more can it happen with abstract concepts?

It is not the word that differs, but rather the thought concept it is meant to symbolize. The only way to make the same word mean the same thing to all men is to subject all people to the selfsame life experience, which is manifestly impossible. Even if it could be done, there is no guarantee that everyone would view the same experiences and occurrences in quite the same way and react alike to the words that symbolize those experiences and occurrences.

Under the circumstances, there is little that can be done to solve the world's semantic problems or to prevent semantics from being enlisted in behalf of a propaganda campaign, which means, basically, getting others to see things the way we want them to see them.

The essence of propaganda is changing people's concepts.

Words are necessary, but they are really only incidental. Words are subject to an iron law of change—in their phonological form, in their structural use, and above all, in their power of symbolization. But the objects and concepts they symbolize are subject to an equally cogent law of change. Hence we have a relationship (or function) between two variables, not between a variable and an invariable. There is no way of systematizing a two-variable relationship. One can only accept it as it appears or occurs at a given moment. One of our semantic difficulties is that we try to stretch out this fleeting instant into an eternity, and "freeze" the relationship.

Propaganda, of one kind or another, will be with us as long as the human race and its languages endure. It is based squarely on semantics, and semantics is the most typically human and rational aspect of language, the one, despite opinions to the contrary, that is language's sole *raison d'être*.

Chapter 4

Studies in Communication

KATHARINE LE MÉE

Communication among persons takes place on many different levels at one time. The words that are spoken and heard are only part of the total exchange of information. Tone of voice, gestures even so small as the blink of an eye and the distance between speakers, all contribute to the meaning conveyed. In recent years much research has been centered on features of communication outside the language process itself but, nevertheless, part of the "semantic ensemble." Paralanguage, gestures, and proxemics are areas of study that group some of these features.

PARALANGUAGE

Nervous coughs, throat-clearing, stuttering or stammering, "uh-huh," the barely audible murmurs that some people make in their throats while listening intently to someone else, drawling speech, excessive loudness or softness, whispering, peculiarities of voice—all these are considerations of *paralanguage* or, as it is also called, *paralinguistics,* from the Greek tonation in phrases such as *"Gosh,* darling! Isn't this *marvelous!"* (in which the italicized syllables would receive the 1) or the kindergarten teacher who takes home the 1–2 intonation used a great deal by small children and says to her husband, "At *rest* hour, *every little boy* and *girl* sits *right* down" (The italicized syllables receiving a 1, which would fade rapidly into a 2).

Very ordinary words may be made to imply almost anything if they are cleverly intoned. A few years ago a popular recording featured a conversation between a young couple that consisted of only two words. The man addressed the woman with her name, "Marcia." She responded with his, "John." Even unimaginative listeners had little trouble in following the progression of the love affair.

Speakers of English are so accustomed to using changes of pitch to indicate shades of meaning that they are surprised to learn that all languages do not operate in quite this way. In languages such as Chinese which are referred to as "tone languages" a change in pitch actually alters the lexical meaning of the word. The Chinese word *li* if pronounced with a rising intonation means *pear;* with a falling intonation, *chestnut.*

Imagine the confusion of a speaker of English has when he attempts to pronounce a Chinese word such as *fu.* These two little sounds may have four different meanings depending on the way they are intoned. If the word is pronounced on the 2 with no variation, the result is *man.* A rise in intonation from 2 to 1 changes the word to *fortune* or *happiness.* If one begins on 4, holds the sound for a bit, and then jumps to 2, the meaning becomes *prefecture.* And, finally, starting on 2 and descending to 4 produces *rich.* An American definitely uses all these intonation patterns. The same word *John* may be pronounced noncommittally (2 held), as a question (2–1), at a distance (4–2), or in a reprimanding manner (2–4). However the word itself does not change its meaning.

In every utterance a certain intonation pattern is normal and expected. One must use the conventional "tune" in order to ask questions, affirm facts, exclaim or demand. But, in addition, one may easily overstep the minimum intonation requirement of the language and color his message in special ways. As soon as a sentence is no longer "bland" or "neutral," as soon as the attitude or emotions of the speaker become apparent, one may say that paralinguistic features are present. An anecdote told by G. K. Chesterton illustrates the *affective* importance of intonation. One day while Mr. Chesterton was walking in a fish market he decided to try a little experiment. Approaching one of the fishwives standing behind the counter, he said in a low-pitched and endearing voice, "You are a noun, a verb, and a preposition." At this well-turned phrase the good woman blushed with apparent pleasure. A little later, after the buying and selling of fish had taken place, Mr. Chesterton tried a different approach. This time he pitched his voice a note higher and ventured, "You are an adjective, an adverb, and a conjunction." At this, she smacked him in the face with a flounder and called the police.

Obviously the fishwife derived meaning from the two remarks. Needless to say, it was not the literal meaning of the words that caused such extraordinary reactions. The woman was so utterly convinced by the tone of Mr. Chesterton's voice that she did not feel it necessary to question what the words meant.

In determining what features are paralinguistic—features that add emotion or attitude—it is important to consider the normal voice of the speaker. Each individual's vocal apparatus differs somewhat from that of others: his vocal cords may be longer or shorter, tenser or more relaxed; his oral and nasal cavities may vary in size and shape; he may be missing several teeth or his teeth may be unevenly spaced— the number of personal factors is very large. These characteristics that differentiate the speech of one individual from that of everyone else are known as "voice set." They are a person's basic vocal equipment.

Many attempts to correlate voice and physical appearance

changed in implication when different accented syllables receive the additional energy of stress:

HE never buys molasses (but perhaps SHE does).
He NEver buys molasses (not even once has he done that).
He never BUYS molasses (someone always gives it to him).
He never buys moLASses (but he does buy honey and sorghum).

Stress becomes a paralinguistic feature whenever speech is extremely loud or soft. Great emotional involvement is usually accompanied by more volume and intensity in the voice, and by violent gestures of the body. Just as pitch may be greatly, appreciably, or slightly overhigh or overlow, stress may be overloud or oversoft in the same degrees. Paralinguistic pitch and stress are not at all confined to a single word or even a single sentence. Rather, they accompany an entire group of sentences giving it all affective meaning.

Juncture

Juncture, a third feature of speech that may be linguistic or paralinguistic, is the way in which the vowels and consonants are joined to each other in the continuum of speech. Sometimes the juncture is very close, the sounds following each other smoothly and in rapid succession. At other times there is a definite pause or hesitation between them. "Nítrate is different from níght ráte"; "gréenhouse from gréen hoúse"; "What do you do with a coúghdrop?" from "What do you do with a coúgh, dróp?" A pause in any utterance tends to emphasize what follows. In the three examples just given, juncture (pause) and accent combine to create a linguistic change in the meaning of the words themselves.

Juncture as a paralinguistic feature is heard in very rapid or very slow speech, or in an irregular pattern in which false starts and hesitations followed by a tumbling of words indicate the troubled emotional state of the speaker.

Other Features

Intonation, stress, and juncture are said to be the condition-ers or qualifiers of speech. Always heard in some degree, they may reveal the extent of emotional involvement. Other para-linguistic characteristics may also be present and may greatly modify the basic voice set and the language itself. Laughing and crying, moaning and groaning, hiccoughing and yawning, are examples. One may continue to talk through these fea-tures. However, others such as coughs, snorts, clicks of the tongue, "uh-huh," "unh-unh," or "shh" are associated with a brief pause. Each language uses these speech noises in its own particular way. Americans use a whole set of them in talking on the telephone. A speaker expects the listener to say "yeh . . . yeh . . . yeh . . . uh-huh . . . yeh" to indicate he's still following the conversation. Sometimes a small throat noise will do. If the listener makes no sound at all, the speaker may be insulted, feeling the other person has stopped listen-ing.

This brief discussion of some paralinguistic features is designed to illustrate some of the ways in which a speaker communicates more than the lexical meaning of his utter-ances. A whole range of information connected with the emo-tional states and attitudes of speaker and listener is also con-veyed. The written language attempts to simulate this by punctuation and typography but is often highly unsuccessful: there is always a feeling of incompleteness, of slight dissatis-faction when one receives a letter from a friend. It is good to "hear" from him but it would be so much better had we heard him with our ears.

The paralinguistic elements that to some extent always ac-company the spoken language are part of the linguistic back-ground of each speaker. Some of these elements are cultural and belong to the community speaking the language, some spirits. The fact that this sort of gesture is learned without the individual's awareness distinguishes it from the "stylized gesture." A young child learns the behavior pattern directly by imitation of others around him. As is true in the acquisition of a first language, a person learns the gestures before he develops to the point of being able to reflect upon them. General cultural gestures are passively known by everyone, but the extent to which they are used depends on an individual's personal tendencies and on the sanctions of his culture. Latin Americans have a great many general cultural gestures and use them exuberantly, whereas the French, who possess a "vocabulary of movement" almost as rich, often hesitate to use it. An attitude of great respect for what is fitting in general, as well as for the "dignity" of the French language in particular, has perhaps caused this restraint. The French apparently consider any addition to or reinforcement of verbal expression to be a mild sort of treason.

Many different types of bodily movement, with purposes as varied as the peoples they represent, may be considered general cultural gestures. For example, pointing is used to indicate or direct attention to a person or object within sight of the speaker. In American culture, when expediency rather than politeness is the first consideration, the index finger acts as the pointer. However this habit is by no means universal; in other groups pointing may be done with eye, nose, or head. Linguists have called attention to what seems to be an unusual phenomenon among the Fox Indians. These people pronounce the *o* of their word *yohi*, "over there," with the lips strongly rounded and protruded. This was puzzling, since the *o* was not pronounced in this manner in other words. Finally it occurred to the observers that these unusual features were not simply a peculiar pronunciation of the sound but were rather a simultaneous pointing.

The French approach everyday matters such as knocking on doors and shaking hands in a way that seems novel to Americans. When knocking, a Frenchman will curve his fin-

gers inward to make a loose fist, and as he taps his palm will be facing himself, not the door. The impression of trying to break into the house is considerably mitigated by this gesture. As soon as the Frenchman shakes hands, however, his movement seems more abrupt. He pumps a friend's hand very energetically but then halts unexpectedly after one shake.

In Spanish-speaking countries a lively gesture is used to indicate that something is neither good nor bad, but simply so-so. The vertically outstretched hand is made to wiggle in a way that suggests the passage of a fish through water. In former times the hand, palm up, stood for "good" in the sense of "nothing hidden," and palm down represented "bad." The wiggle is said, therefore, to represent a sort of vacillation between the two opposites. It is easy to see that general cultural gestures may also refer to ideas, persons, or objects not present at the time.

Often the motion used is a direct representation, a drawing in air, of what is being referred to. An American indicates the height of an object by extending his hand, palm down, at the proper level. A Latin American also shows height (of an animal at least) by using his outstretched hand, but with a noticeable variation: the hand is extended vertically with the thumb up, rather than horizontally. If, however, he is speaking of a person, he is likely to show height by using his upright forefinger.

A Frenchman might ask you to have a drink with him by making a gesture in which the right hand is clenched and the thumb, symbolizing the neck of the bottle, is jerked toward the mouth. When times are tough and he can barely afford "to throw one in back of his tie," as the French expression goes, he may pretend to tighten his belt in a gesture of deprivation and mock suffering.

If the same Frenchman wishes to indicate that something is first class, he will not represent number one by using his index finger, as Americans do, but will use his thumb instead. This is to be expected, since the French habitually start counting with the thumb and go on to the index finger for number two.

Of special interest are "euphemistic" general cultural gestures. French and English have exchanged *les waters* and *toilet,* expressions that mean the same thing but have presumably gained social approval by coming from a foreign source. In the same way gestures may often be used in place of speech when the idea communicated is concerned with superstition, sexual relationships, mental defects, drunkenness, and the like. Latin Americans use a colorful gesture to forestall evil:

the middle and ring fingers of the left hand are turned against the palm and held down with the thumb while the index and little finger are extended to represent a horseshoe, symbolic of good luck. Here, then, the gesture mimes the symbol supposed to invoke good fortune. An identical gesture in Italian is called *fare le corna,* "to point the horns," and is supposed to ward off the evil eye.

If it is money that the individual lacks rather than good fortune, Latin Americans typically use a gesture called *estar a dos velas,* "to be with two candles." The person places the right index finger and the middle finger on either side of the nose and then draws the two downward. These fingers represent the two candles that are left to burn in the sanctuary of a church once the service is over. Since the candles are small and not very generous with their light, they represent the penniless individual. A common gesture for stealing used in Mexico, Colombia, and Venezuela is made by extending the fingers like claws and then bending the first and second joints inward as if to scratch something.

The general cultural gesture does not always "draw" or represent objects or symbols. Very often it is purely arbitrary and conventional within a given culture. If it had a meaning historically, this meaning is no longer recognized by the people who use the gesture. No one can show any logical connection between the movement and the concept it represents. Why, for example, does a gentleman remove his hat in the presence of a lady or when he enters a room? What is the significance of knocking on wood or crossing one's fingers for good luck? Then, too, there are the various ways different peoples use their heads to indicate "no." Americans, of course, use the horizontal nod; but in certain East Mediterranean areas a negative reply consists of a click accompanied by a sharp lift of the head and eyebrows. In still other cultures, among the Malayan Negritos for instance, the idea of negation is communicated by casting down the eyes. A person must be initiated into the ways of the particular culture in order to understand these gestures. The native is taught them by his society, and he masters them as he does his first language, by imitation and without specific awareness of what he is doing. These gestures may also be consciously learned by the foreigner, but here very often, as for the spoken language, there is an "accent" that marks him as a stranger, a certain awkwardness that betrays a different background. A similar phenomenon may be observed within a society when people appears that one wishes the other to do her a favor—something small but nevertheless bothersome. In explaining her predicament, the first lady, with a burst of apparent enthusiasm, leans close to the second, almost physically pressing her with the urgency of her request. The observer who does not hear the words exchanged between the two nevertheless notices that as one woman approaches, the other moves back, that the two, though proceeding fairly slowly, are nevertheless covering ground; one retires, the other follows. A few days later, the observer, in conversation with the more passive of the two, hears her say, "You know, I met Mrs. X the other day, and she wanted me to do something for her. I'm sure it must have been something I could have done easily, but I couldn't really hear her talking. She was standing so close to me, practically breathing in my face. I was so anxious to move away that I made any sort of excuse just to be free." The conversation had been terminated abruptly and the favor had gone undone; both parties went away feeling uncomfortable and somewhat annoyed—all because a very subtle and invisible barrier between the two women had been overstepped.

This incident is of small consequence. We might dismiss the example by saying simply that Mrs. X is unduly pushy. But it does illustrate, as most of us will agree after a small amount of observation, that the space between people must be correctly adjusted to the situation for both parties to feel at ease.

Within the past fifteen or twenty years a great amount of research has been devoted to all aspects of the communication process—to the sounds (vowels and consonants) people make when speaking, to such features as pitch, intensity, and intonation with which they modify the stream of sounds, and to the posture and movements of their bodies. Recently the emphasis has been extended away from the body itself to the area immediately surrounding it. This new study of the ways in which people of different cultures relate to and organize the space around them is called proxemics. The name comes from a Latin word *proximus* meaning "nearest in space" and a Greek suffix *-ics*, "pertaining to," which is used in the names of many other sciences.

The scholar perhaps most responsible for advances in this field is Edward T. Hall, professor of anthropology at Illinois Institute of Technology. His book *The Silent Language*[1] is a fascinating study of the ways in which different cultures may be compared. His latest work, *The Hidden Dimension*,[2] complements the first and addresses itself specifically to the question at hand here, namely man's use of space. In presenting this summary we have drawn upon some of Dr. Hall's acute observations of the Arabic culture.

One of the primary purposes of proxemics is to enlarge our abilities to perceive first, and then to understand, the people, objects, and events we see. The story is told of a Frenchman who came to the United States on a tour of inspection of industrial plants. From the very beginning his American hosts felt that he was faintly displeased, but after repreated questioning they still had failed to find out what was troubling him. Finally when the end of the tour was nearing, the Frenchman finally blurted out, "Why do you talk so much about free enterprise, when all your industries are nationalized?" The Americans, amazed that such a conclusion could have been drawn, hastened to explain that it was not so and then to question the source of this unexpected observation. At first the Frenchman could not remember what had created his very strong impression. Finally, days later, he recalled the particular thing that had so amazed him: each American factory he had seen had prominently displayed the American flag from its roof. In France the presence of the national tricolor always indicates that the industry is government-controlled.

Very similar objects may not have the same meaning in every culture. Not only is the idea evoked by a given thing different, but also the degree of importance assigned to it.

[1] New York: Doubleday, 1959.
[2] New York: Doubleday, 1966.

Take, for instance, window shutters, which many Americans add as decoration or as a finishing touch to their houses. Occasionally, when the sun is especially penetrating or when the weather is exceptionally bad, these shutters become functional and are closed. However, most of the time, day or night, they are left open. It is interesting to note how the French use their shutters, or *volets*. The windows of a French house are generally not of the typical American "guillotine type," which slam down, often at the slightest provocation. They are casement windows, with two vertical sides that open at the center, and unlike American windows, are usually unencumbered by screens. From within the room, a person may easily swing the windows inside and then reach out to the *volets*. A typical Frenchman feels that, come sunset, the *volets* should be tightly closed. *On ne vit pas devant tout le monde* ("One does not live in front of everybody") is his attitude. He feels there is a very sharp division between what is exterior to the family circle and what is interior, and he does not wish to share any aspect of his private life with his neighbors. The American traveler or guest, on the other hand, feels stifled. He is accustomed to more openness. At his home windows are left wide open in summer and it is not uncommon to see into the living or dining room from the outside. Being suddenly surrounded by closed shutters is somewhat oppressive. The American is likely to feel that the French are being secretive or that they have something to hide, though it is unlikely that this is true.

A Frenchman's house and property as a whole are also evidence of his preference for privacy. As one walks down a street one can see quite clearly where the domain of each family begins and ends, because of the placement of substantial fences on the division lines. These barriers are about waist-high and are sometimes locked with a key. A visitor often must ring a bell at the barrier to be admitted to the property. Walls between properties are not uncommon and, topped with spikes or broken glass, they are generally constructed to be respected. How different this is from America, where in small towns lawn runs into lawn and dog meets dog without the interruption of a fence.

Even in French cemeteries the division between perpetual properties still exists. Each plot is very clearly and symmetrically delineated by a surrounding stone or metal divider, often six or eight inches high. Families who cannot afford this type of barrier will often separate their plot from their neighbors' by using small bushes or shrubs. The effect is one of a small, self-contained garden.

The traveler immediately notes certain differences in the arrangement and use of various objects in a foreign country. It is to be hoped that he gains, also, an insight into the diversities of the human beings who use them. Those who assume that "people are people" no matter where one goes not only miss an enriching experience of learning, but, in their gaucheness, offend the very people with whom they seek a common bond.

Research in proxemics has led to clear illustrations of a very important fact: an individual may be bound by his culture as far as his perceptions are concerned. Very simply this means that his society has taught him how to look, to speak, to smell, to touch, and even to arrange himself in certain spatial relationships with other people. Some examples can help demonstrate this fact.

Let us return to the matter of conversation between two or several people, since this is a situation easily observed and full of information about human behavior. If an Englishman and an American are speaking together, the chances are good that the first is looking the second squarely in the eye. English culture teaches that politeness demands this sort of attentive gaze. The American, on the other hand, has been taught that it is impolite to stare. His eyes are probably wandering to the side unless he wants to make a particularly forceful point, whereupon he looks his interlocutor briefly in the eye. The Englishman has also been taught to speak softly, that is, at a volume which reaches only the ears of his listener. Any raising of the voice is considered an intrusion on the other people in the room. However, the American, with his characteristic desire to show that all is honest and forthright (whether it is or not), tends to speak louder and louder as he becomes more and more involved in the conversation. The result is that the American goes away feeling that the Englishman is timid and lacks forcefulness; the Englishman feels that the American is somewhat shifty and quite rude.

The matter of when to speak and when not to often causes cross-cultural misunderstandings. Dr. Hall tells of a young Arab student who was studying with an American family. At one point the family became very distressed with him and gave him what Americans call "the silent treatment." The Arab had no way of knowing that he was being reprimanded, for in his culture silence is often natural and expected. Arabs do not feel it necessary to gain privacy by placing a physical barrier between themselves and others. Instead of moving to another room, they simply fall silent. For this reason the student never responded to what his American hosts regarded as a broad hint.

If one considers two other senses, those of touching and smelling, one is amazed again at cross-cultural diversity. People of a given culture may be thought of as surrounded by a private and of course invisible bubble. Its inside is private territory; others should not enter. The size of this bubble is culturally determined. For Americans it is quite large, since, in general, we avoid close contact with strangers; for other peoples, Latin Americans for example, it is much smaller. Evidence of this feeling for what constitutes "one's own space" is not difficult to find: the American who deals with Latin Americans may purposely install a wide desk to oblige the person being interviewed to "keep his distance." Some have gone so far as to have immovable chairs placed in the room before the beginning of an interview.

Americans stand back in other ways also, particularly in

contrast with the French. The French are constantly shaking hands with their friends and colleagues: a white-collar worker would not think of beginning his daily activities without this token of friendly recognition for every single person in his office, nor would he leave at the end of the day without repeating the ritual. As the occasion becomes more social one is even more careful of this detail. It is considered quite rude, for example, to leave a party or wedding reception without taking leave in this very personal manner of every guest present, whether or not he is a close friend. It is noteworthy, too, that in France, as well as in most other Western countries, women shake hands when they are introduced to someone. In the United States this amenity is usually limited to men.

Another pleasant detail of French social behavior, which amazes Americans and which takes a bit of courage and adaptation on their part, is the frequency of kissing. Children are taught very early to make the rounds, placing a kiss on each cheek of all the members of the family every time they return to or go away from home. This habit is not lost in adolescence; it is not at all unusual to see French teen-agers, boys and girls, kiss each other and shake hands before taking leave. Even adult men are seen embracing each other and walking arm in arm, particularly in the South of France.

As far as the sense of smell is concerned, Americans go through procedures that strike many other peoples as highly unnatural if not completely ridiculous. We do our best, with the aid of air deodorizers and air-conditioning and purifying apparatuses, to render our environment as free from odor, as "hygienic" as possible. An American woman, once she has availed herself of toothpaste, hairspray, deodorant, hand and body lotions, scented face powder, and other cosmetics, has admirably succeeded in masking the natural human odor which is considered highly desirable in other parts of the world. An Arab, for instance, in choosing a marriage partner for his son, is likely to want to know how the lady in question smells. This criterion is important since Arabs live in much closer contact with each other than do Americans. According to Dr. Hall, Arabs like to almost bathe each other in breath, a custom that Americans find extremely repugnant.

People of certain societies often show a very high development of one or more senses as a result of the environmental conditions in which they live. An Eskimo can travel for one hundred or more miles over a snowy terrain without landmarks. Evidently this unique ability comes from the fact that he can feel differences in the direction and smell of the wind, and can detect subtle changes in the ice and snow on which he walks.

This training to perceive the world in different ways is reflected in how people place themselves with respect to other people and in how they arrange their belongings. As a commonplace example, consider the fact that Americans will, almost without fail, avoid the first row of seats in a schoolroom or church. To take these places would make us feel isolated, a bit too "eager beaver," and would deprive us of the opportunity of seeing how others are reacting to the situation. In Germany, however, the attitude is different. Students there prize the first seats and by sitting so close to the professor they show their interest in and enthusiasm for the subject being taught. American college students tend to be casual both with regard to the professor and to the material being studied, and this attitude is reflected in their posture and in how they dress. The slouch, the sweatshirts and blue jeans or bermuda shorts that sometimes characterize the "intellectual fatigúe" in our midst find no place in European schools. The psychological distance between student and professor is very great, and an attitude, both physical and mental, of respect and attention prevails.

Dr. Hall in *The Hidden Dimension* makes some enlightening observations on the behavior of Americans and Arabs in public places. For example, when Americans go to places such as a theater, a classroom, or a public waiting room, they generally lay claim to the available seats on a first-come, first-served basis; latecomers respect the priority of those who arrived first and do not try to interfere. However, another attitude seems to prevail among the Arabs, namely, that public areas are really "public" and no one has any particular claim to them, even for a brief period of time. With this in mind it is not difficult to see why the last rows of theaters in Beirut are very unpopular places to sit. If the auditorium is crowded, the standees will try to sit down even though the seats are already occupied. The result is that the hardy ones remain; others give in and leave.

The French have patterns of spatial arrangement that turn up quite persistently in many different ways. One of these is a fondness for the "spider web"—the control in the center connected to the periphery by several strong strands that are, themselves, joined by weaker threads. Anyone who has visited Paris has seen an example of this in Place de l'Etoile, where twelve streets converge at a central arch. Travelers in France who are in a hurry find it much easier to begin their trip at the capital, from which all major rail and auto routes emanate, than to try to make good connections from town to town.

Any American or Englishman visiting France cannot help but be struck by another aspect of spatial arrangement, the tendency of the French to strive for absolute symmetry. Whereas an English garden is a carefree, natural mingling of colors and shapes, the French one is neatly trimmed and stylized with the whole pattern in mind. A striking example can be found along the Loire River, at the chateau of Villandry: the gardens of thick bushes and low shrubs are exquisitely cut to provide visual symbols of the various kinds of love—divine, passionate, courtly—of the Renaissance. In public places in France the foreigner's curiosity is apt to be aroused by plates of flowers, about the size of a charcoal broiler, raised on a tripod. The small flowers arranged to form a fleur-de-lis or other design are never even slightly out of line. One is charmed by the display of delicateness and precision.

Patterns such as the ones described here contribute to a country's culture, in the broadest sense of that word. Individuals acquire the characteristic manner of arranging themselves and their possessions from the society around them. The learning takes place at a very young age, sometimes by imitation, sometimes under pressure to conform encouraged by adults. These patterns of behavior are as characteristic of a country as its language or gestures. Proxemics orders and explains data about the display of persons and objects in space so that cross-cultural diversity may be appreciated and not misunderstood.

Chapter 5

What's Happened to Grammar?
—A Historical Survey of Grammars
in America

DON L. F. NILSEN

After taking a course in Latin, people are sometimes heard to say that only now, after studying Latin grammar, can they understand English grammar. This is not because of the similarity between English and Latin, but because many of the definitions and concepts of the kind of traditional grammar that is taught in schools are based on Greek and Latin grammars. Karl Dykema and Charles Hartung are only two of many authors who have been able to give ample support for this contention. For the purposes of this essay, however, the fact that our early grammars were largely dependent on Latin and Greek grammars is not as important as the result of this dependence. In the American schoolrooms of the eighteenth, nineteenth, and even twentieth century, a noun was the name of a person, place, or thing; a verb was a word expressing action or state of being; an adjective was something that modified a noun or pronoun or that answered the question Which? What kind of? How many?; a pronoun was something that took the place of a noun—and so on through the traditional parts of speech.

As proof of the effectiveness of this kind of teaching, teachers would point out that their better students would almost always agree when identifying the parts of speech in a piece of writing, not realizing that the students might be arriving at the correct answers in spite of the definitions rather than because of them. After all, in the teaching process, the definitions were always supplemented by numerous examples—enough examples, in fact, that a good student would perhaps unconsciously arrive at his own working definition by generalizing from the examples.

It was the structural-descriptive linguists who in the 1930's began pointing out that the definitions were inconsistent, some being based on meaning (a verb expresses action or state of being), some on function (an adverb modifies an adjective or another adverb), and some on distribution (a pronoun takes the place of a noun). It was these linguists who also pointed out the special weaknesses of the meaning-based definitions by showing that even nonsense words can be identified as one part of speech or another by observing how they relate to other words in a sentence. Thus *fretish* is a noun in *I like to drink fretish whenever I watch TV;* it is a verb in *I would rather fretish on Wednesdays than on Tuesdays;* and it is an adjective in *The object was as fretish as any I've seen.* It is surely obvious to most people that *fretish* is a verb in the second sentence, but not in the first or third. A structural linguist would ask how the reader, who does not know the meaning of *fretish* (which has no meaning), knows that the second *fretish* shows action or state of being. The inescapable conclusion is that the reader cannot be using the conventional meaning-based definition of verb in calling *fretish* a verb.

These structural-descriptive linguists (or scientific linguists, as they liked to call themselves) also objected to the "doctrine of correctness" that traditional grammarians subscribed to. The traditionalists had set up a hypothetical "correct" English that they attempted to teach their students. Following the example of traditional scholars such as Otto Jespersen, Henrik Poutsma, and Etsko Kruisinga, the schoolbook grammarians selected and analyzed sentences from literature that had had time to become well established and respected. This often resulted in the sample sentences being far removed in time, as well as geography, from the language that the students would meet in their homes and communities, in newspapers and magazines, on radio and television, and even in current literature. In 1966 when this author was teaching a college grammar class, he found the prescribed textbook analyzing such sentences as *Whither thou goest, I will go,* and *My son, if sinners entice thee, consent thou not.*

Probably traditional grammarians should not be criticized for attempting to teach what they considered the best English, but rather for not recognizing (or at least for not treating) the fact that all English is not alike. They analyzed formal written English and from this made rules which teachers tried to apply to all English, whether it was that spoken in the pomp and ceremony of a Presidential inauguration, or that spoken in the heat and confusion of branding time on a New Mexico cattle ranch.

It is ironic that in recent decades most English teachers have been expected to teach literature as well as "correct" English, and in teaching literature—not just sample sentences —the teachers found that they were constantly being faced with examples of what the grammar book called "bad English." Some of the best writers ended their sentences with prepositions and used double superlatives and split infinitives, for example.

English teachers were faced with a contradiction between what they met in their grammar books and what they met elsewhere, because their grammars were based only partly on accurate observations. Some of the rules of usage were included in the grammars simply because they had been an unquestioned part of such books for a hundred and fifty years. In first composing these rules, eighteenth-century school grammarians such as George Campbell, Robert Lowth, Lindley Murray, and Joseph Priestley naturally relied on the well-formulated rules of Latin (which was then thought to be the ideal language); hence the rules about not ending sentences with prepositions and not splitting infinitives. For their original intuitive statements, they based their analysis on the semantics or meaning of words; hence the emphasis on logic in language such as in the rule against double negatives. Sometimes these grammarians made innovations of their own in an attempt to improve the language. A classic example is the complicated rule which states that *shall* should be used with the first person, and *will* should be used with the second and third person; that is, unless a special effect (emphasis, for example) is desired, in which case the rule is reversed.

The traditional grammarians were very thorough in teaching their doctrine of correctness, and evidence of their success can often be observed even outside the schools. A prominent television personality recently waged a campaign against highway sign painters because their signs read *Slow* rather than *Slowly*. And while the author was preparing this essay, the following letter appeared in the nationally syndicated "Dear Abby" column:

Dear Abby:
I was profoundly shaken to read in your column the following sentence:
"She sounds like she could have hunted bear with a switch."
Abby, how sad that you, too, have sunk to the level where you would introduce a clause with the preposition "like."
Apparently your command of basic English has also been corrupted and debased by those relentless destroyers of English grammar—the writers of radio and television commercials. Now my faith in your judgment in all matters is in grave jeopardy.

The tone of this criticism is much the same as that received by editors of *Webster's Third New International Dictionary*. People were offended at the dictionary because it did not carefully prescribe usage as a traditionally edited dictionary would do. Furthermore, it included items from many levels of usage, and the editors chose not to pass judgment on many items that more traditional dictionaries would have labeled substandard or not have included at all. Under the structural philosophy, people had come to expect that a description of language would include a description of the user or the situation calling for a particular word or structure.

Describing or classifying certain aspects of language as being typical of the "cultured and well educated," of the "young, modern, and somewhat educated," or of the "old-fashioned, rustic, and poorly educated" is only one small part of what the structuralists attempted to do. Under the leadership of Leonard Bloomfield, they separated language into two divisions: syntax and semantics (semantics relates to meaning, syntax to form or structure). The model that received the greatest degree of acceptance for the study of the syntactic component was provided by Charles C. Fries of the University of Michigan. The new system was more consistent than the old because its definitions, and therefore its part-of-speech identifications, were based entirely on positional distribution. Thus a noun could be identified as a noun by noting where it occurred in relation to other words in a sentence—preceded by various kinds of noun modifiers and determiners, preceded by a preposition, followed by a verb, etc. On the basis of such distributional information, "test frames" with "slots" were devised, such as "The _____ is/are good," for defining the various parts of speech. The structuralists pointed out that it is distributional clues that allow grammarians to correctly identify the part of speech of the nonsense word *fretish* in *I like to drink fretish whenever I watch TV, I would rather fretish on Wednesdays than on Tuesdays,* and *The object was as fretish as any I've seen*; and it is likewise distributional clues, and not the traditional definitions, that allow them to correctly identify the part of speech of regular words that have meaning.

In addition to their formal grammar, the structuralists made a significant contribution in changing attitudes toward language. The way was paved for them by historical linguists who discovered that Latin was not the "parent" language, but along with many other languages had descended from what the historians termed Indo-European. In light of this, the structuralists reevaluated standards of usage. They pointed out that language is not permanently set, but is a living and changing phenomenon. They convinced many people that speech was primary and that the written language is only a representation of speech. They showed how each language is unique, and therefore a grammar of one language cannot serve as the grammar of another. One of their most basic beliefs and teachings was that the speakers and users of a language dictate the language. All these ideas increased people's respect for the language they met in everyday life.

Fewer college professors felt it necessary to have their correspondence checked for grammar by their colleagues in the English department. At cocktail parties and grocery stores, English teachers found that a gradually increasing number of people would converse with them—even after learning their occupation. Suddenly committee members found it not quite as difficult to get celebrities to speak to conventions of English teachers. And perhaps best of all, English teachers began to listen to their fellow man with an ear for content, rather than grammar.

But critics point out that on the other hand, a generation already indifferent to the subtleties of English was lulled into complacency and carelessness. The structuralists as keepers of the language were compared to errant gardeners who sat idly by, conversing about the beauties of nature, while their immaculate and well-disciplined garden returned to chaos and wilderness.

People on both sides of the controversy agree that the structuralists were successful in destroying the unquestioned faith in the old doctrine of correctness. But it is interesting that the structuralists treated only the comments about usage and the explanations that accompanied the analysis of sentences. They mainly ignored the fact that the traditionalists developed an objective, formal, and rigorous system for describing sentences—in fact two systems. The structuralists were certainly not the first to notice that words systematically contrasted with other words. The traditionalists had used paradigms such as the following:

		NOMINATIVE	POSSESSIVE	OBJECTIVE
1st Person		I	my	me
2nd Person		you	your	you
3rd Person	Masc.	he	his	him
	Fem.	she	her	her
	Neut.	it	its	it

And although the structuralists criticized the traditional paradigms as being based too much on Latin and Greek—as some indeed were—those structuralists who have specialized in comparative and historical linguistics also make extensive use of paradigms, with modifications where warranted.

The other formal system that was devised by the traditionalists was diagramming. Stephen Clark in 1851 was one of the first to publish a system of diagramming. His diagrams looked very much like the present ones except that he drew elliptical balloons around the various words rather than placing them on lines. About twenty-five years after Clark's book was published, Reed and Kellogg published a system of diagrams based on Clark's, but revised to much the same as the one used by traditionalists today. It is noteworthy that until recently the structuralists seem to have ignored traditional diagrams. The rigor and objectivity of the traditional diagrams was their foremost strength; it was also, however, their most obvious weakness because the diagrams were testable statements and it could be seen that they did not always present accurate or complete information. A traditional diagram would not analyze a verb cluster such as *might have been being stolen,* which consists of five separate words and nine separate morphemes. (A morpheme is defined by structuralists as the smallest element that has meaning. *Being,* for instance, consists of two morphemes—*be* and *-ing.* Although most people would not think of *-ing* as having meaning, to the grammarian it means "happening now.") The traditional diagram does not treat these morphemes, nor does it show the relationship between the active and passive voices. For example, to make an active sentence passive, both the past participle ending and a form of the verb *be* must be inserted into the sentence, with the *be* form preceding the past participle. *John took the book* changes in the passive to *The book was taken by John.* When a word has more than one function in a sentence (for example, if it is subject of the main verb and object of an infinitive), the traditional diagram can indicate only one of the functions.

Although traditional diagrams do account for some deleted elements, such as the understood *you* in an imperative sentence, modern grammarians expect much more than this. They want a grammar that can consistently trace deletions so that the structural difference between such phrases as *baby bottle* and *baby salamander* can be shown, and the ambiguity in a sentence like *The teen-agers of today are shocking world citizens* can be traced. They also expect a grammar to show the relationship between related structures such as *Ann visited us tonight, Ann's visiting us tonight, For Ann to visit us tonight.* In addition, modern grammarians want not only to analyze sentences that have already been written, but to have a system that can be used to create or generate sentences.

Neither the traditional nor the structural models filled the above requirements completely. In the 1950's a new grammatical system emerged under the leadership of Noam Chomsky. It is called *generative* grammar because at its core is the basic belief that a grammar should be creative; it should synthesize or generate sentences rather than merely analyze them. It is also called *transformational* because it shows relationships between structures, that is, the way one structure is changed or transformed into another.

It is generally acknowledged among linguists that the generative model has important roots in the structural model, and that it even analyzes many sentences—the kernel, or basic, sentences—by using structural concepts and techniques. Less often realized is that the generative model also has important roots in traditional grammar, and that it probably relies more on traditional grammar than does structural grammar, which tried to discard as much as possible of the traditional.

In order to compare the three methods of analysis let us take a sentence that includes a rather complex verb cluster (*Have been being used*) and a nonsensical noun phrase (**the inhaled chairs*). (The asterisk shows that the phrase is, according to the linguist, deviant, or in the transformationalist's terms, "ungrammatical." The purpose of using such a phrase in our example will become evident below.) The traditional grammarian would diagram the sentence *Haven't the inhaled chairs been being used all morning?* somewhat like this:

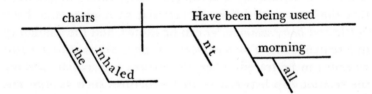

And the structural grammarian of the Fries persuasion would diagram the same sentence somewhat like this:

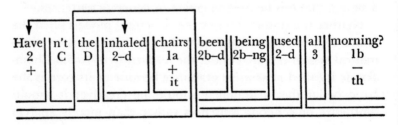

Both of these diagrams indicate that the sentence consists of two parts—*the inhaled chairs* and *Haven't been being used all morning*. Furthermore, both diagrams show that *the inhaled chairs, Haven't been being used,* and *all morning* are phrases, that is, groups of words interacting closely with each other. The traditional diagram indicates that *chairs* and *Have been being used* are more important than the other words by diagramming them on the base line, though this information is not given in the structural diagram, and indeed, it is perhaps disputable that the word *Have,* for example, is more important than the word *morning.*

The traditional diagram indicates what is functioning as subject (*chairs*), and what is functioning as predicate (*Have been being used*); it indicates that *chairs* has two modifiers (*the* and *inhaled*), and the crooked line under *inhaled* indicates that this modifier is derived from a verb, though it is functioning as a modifier in this particular sentence. It shows that *n't* is modifying the verb cluster, and that *all morning* is doing the same, but the fact that *all morning* is diagrammed as the object of an unstated preposition indicates that *all morning* is an adverbial complement. And it shows us that *all* modifies *morning.* The fact that *Have* is capitalized indicates that the sentence is interrogative, as only interrogative sentences begin with the first word in the verb cluster. The diagram indicates that the grammatical relationships in *Haven't the inhaled chairs been being used all morning?* are exactly the same as those in *The inhaled chairs haven't been being used all morning.*, because these two sentences are diagrammed exactly the same way except for capitalization; the diagram, therefore, can show relationships between related structures.

It would seem that subject, predicate, and complement are important enough to be set off. Generally, the traditional diagram does this well; however, traditional grammarians do not have a simple predicate (parallel to simple subject as contrasted with complete subject), and therefore the traditional diagram does not show the verb phrase as containing any structure. In our example the words *Have been being used* are merely diagrammed as a verb cluster, even though the cluster contains four different words and seven morphemes—*Have, be, -en, be, -ing, use,* and *-ed*—and even though one of these morphemes, *use,* is more basic than all the others. Complements are also inadequately treated in traditional diagramming. For example, *on the table* in *Her hand is on the table* and in *She put her hand on the table* is diagrammed as a simple verb modifier, although it is a subjective complement in the first and an objective complement in the second.

The structural diagram does not consider certain words more important than others. It leaves the words in the same order in which they were uttered or written, and it begins by classifying the words. The words are first classed into two major categories, depending on whether they are more important in signaling semantic or grammatical meaning. Those that signal mainly semantic meaning—roughly the nouns, verbs, adjectives, and adverbs—are called *form words,* and are given a number designation: 1, 2, 3, and 4 respectively. Those that signal mainly grammatical meaning—the articles, auxiliaries, negatives, intensifiers, conjunctions—are called *function words* and are given letter designations: A, B, C, D, and E respectively.

Although it is not always obvious whether a word is a form word or a function word, this seems to be a useful distinction. There are a number of important differences between form words and function words: (1) Form words are dependent on the subject of discourse while function words are not; for example, a composition about cows might contain the word *milk* fifty times while a composition about school buildings might not contain the word *milk* at all. On the other hand, the function word *the* would probably occur about an equal number of times in each composition. (2) Form-word categories are limitless, whereas function-word categories are not; for example, it would not be difficult to list every conjunction in English, but it would be impossible to list every noun. (3)

Form words can take endings that signal the category to which they belong—for example, *-s, -ed, -en, -ing* for verbs; *-ly, -er, -est* for adverbs and adjectives—while function words cannot. (4) Form words in English change freely from one category to another (especially between noun and verb), while function words do not.

In our example we have a Class *2* word, followed by a *C,* and a *D,* and a Class *2* plus an ending, followed by Class *1,* etc. The *a* after the *1* of the fifth word and the *b* after the *1* of the last word indicate that these two words do not refer to the same thing. If they had the same referent, they would both be *1a.* Below the classification number or figure, there are plus signs or minus signs. The plus indicates that the word is plural (*Have* and *chairs*), and the minus indicates that the word is singular (*morning*). This is important for determining what is the subject and what is the verb: the first Class *1* word and Class *2* word that have the same number designation, in the case of our sentence *Have* (+), and *chairs* (+). The fact that the Class *1* word and Class *2* word are inverted, with the Class *2* word coming first, signals that this sentence is a question. After the words have been categorized and the concordance noted, the sentence structure can be observed by noting the categories and their relations to each other.

The structural method is objective and rigorous, and although it does not display the various relationships as well as does traditional diagramming, it has the advantage of telling precisely to which category each word belongs, giving more information about word endings, and giving more information about sentence types.

In order to determine the sentence type, one looks at the basic structure; the following might be examples of sentence types:

TYPE	STRUCTURE	EXAMPLE
I	1a 2	John swims.
II	1a 2 1a	John became captain.
III	1a 2 1b	John hit his wife.

| IV | 1a 2 1b 1c | John gave his wife a gift. |
| V | 1a 2 1b 1b | John considers his wife a fool. |

It should be noted that the traditional diagrams can also be used to distinguish one sentence type from another. For example, in terms of traditional diagrams, the five types above would be described as follows:

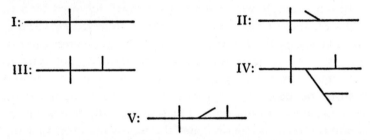

I: II:

III: IV:

V:

But now let us consider a grammar that is different both from traditional and from structural, and let us see what information this grammar gives that traditional and structural grammars do not give. And more important, let us see if this additional information is of any value, especially from the pedagogical point of view. In the first place, it should be noted that both the structural and the traditional models began with an actual sentence, and then through different techniques analyzed the sentence. The generative-transformational model does not begin with the words that compose the sentence, but rather with grammatical terms that gradually get closer and closer to the actual words.

Our example, *Haven't the inhaled chairs been being used all morning?*, contains two basic, or kernel, sentences: *Someone used the chairs all morning* and the deviant *Someone inhales the chairs*. The second sentence is inserted, or imbedded, into the first, and then certain "transforms" are applied. A diagram (usually called a *tree*) of the basic kernel sentence would look like the upper part of this diagram. One transformational rule is that every English noun can be modified by a sentence transformed into a relative clause, etc. This is how the second sentence is imbedded into the first:

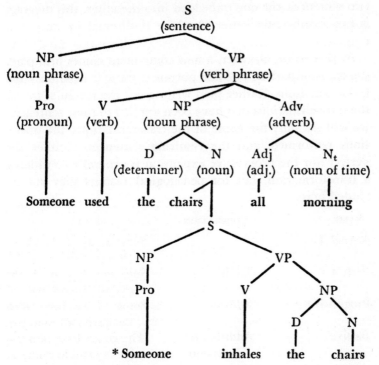

Thus the generative grammarian, like the structural grammarian, views sentence structure as a hierarchy. But unlike the structural grammarian, he begins with the most abstract concept and systematically makes his way down to the more concrete levels until he has generated the actual words of the sentence. Going from sentence to noun phrase plus verb phrase, and on down this diagram, each division point, or *node*, is given a name, and this name is used for the unit from that point down, whether the unit is a single word, a phrase, or a clause. Thus, *chairs* is a noun; *the chairs* is a noun phrase; *inhales the chairs* is a verb phrase; and *someone inhales the chairs* is a sentence. But *inhales the* does not have a node and therefore does not have a name, nor are these two words functioning together as a unit—either as phrase or clause. But other than showing this and showing the relationship between the two sentences, the one imbedded into the other, this diagram is not significantly better than the traditional or structural diagrams.

At this point, however, a new component comes into play: the transformation. For our purposes, we will need only ten transformations. Rather than writing out the formulas for all the transformations that have been applied to these sentences, we will list only the name of the transformations, the operations performed, and the resulting sentences. Neither the perfect nor the progressive expansion is generally considered a transformation, but for pedagogical reasons they are included here.

NAME	OPERATION	RESULT
Kernel 1		Someone used the chairs all morning.
Perfect	Addition	Someone has used the chairs all morning.
Progressive	Addition	Someone has been using the chairs all morning.
Passive	Addition & Inversion	The chairs have been being used all morning by someone.
Agent Deletion	Deletion	The chairs have been being used all morning.
Negation	Addition	The chairs haven't been being used all morning.
Question	Inversion	Haven't the chairs been being used all morning?
Kernel 2		*Someone inhales the chairs.
Passive	Addition & Inversion	*The chairs are inhaled by someone.
Agent Deletion	Deletion	*The chairs are inhaled.
Relative	Substitution & (Inversion)	*which are inhaled
Relative + *be* Deletion	Deletion	*inhaled

After embedding Kernel 2 into Kernel 1 as shown in the generative-transformational diagram, and inverting the noun and modifier (since in English a single-word past participle modifying a noun must precede that noun), the following sentence results: *Haven't the inhaled chairs been being used all morning?* Since the insert sentence is deviant, the resultant sentence is also deviant. In the kernel-generating component of the generative-transformational model, this sentence could not be generated because the verb *inhales* requires that a gaseous substance be the direct object. This deviant example is used for two purposes: first, it shows that if the kernel is deviant, then all of the sentences derived from that kernel will be deviant in exactly the same way; and second, this model shows not only *that* the structure is deviant, but also *why* it is deviant—*inhaled chairs* is deviant because *Someone inhales chairs* is deviant, and that is deviant because of the incongruence between verb and direct object.

Thus, the generative grammarian has a technique for generating kernel sentences, and has transformations that will make these kernel sentences passive, interrogative, negative, etc. He also has other transformations that will make them into phrases or words and embed them into other sentences in various ways.

Although traditional grammarians have had no formal machinery to show that a sentence such as *John ate the cake* is related to *The cake was eaten by John,* they have long been interested in such relationships. The transformational component is nothing more than the formal machinery necessary for showing such relationships. It is true that this added machinery makes the grammar more complicated (the sample sentence was more complex than most), but transformationalists feel this complication is justified by the added insights that are derived.

One of the most important insights that the transformational component gives is the concept of deep structure as opposed to surface structure. In order to explain this concept, let us assume that there are two types of transformations—those that do not change meaning, and those that do change meaning but in a consistent way. Let us call the first set, *paraphrase* transformations, and the second set *nonparaphrase* transformations. It is paraphrase transformations that relate the sentences in Column A to those in Column B:

COLUMN A	COLUMN B	TRANSFORMATION
John recovered the stolen goods.	The stolen goods were recovered by John.	Passive
Mary tried on the bikini.	Mary tried the bikini on.	Separation
Several boys were eating apples.	There were several boys eating apples.	Expletive
The left fielder caught the ball confidently.	Confidently the left fielder caught the ball.	Adverb Inversion
	The left fielder confidently caught the ball.	Adverb Inversion 2
I gave a car to my wife.	I gave my wife a car.	Indirect-object Inversion
I remained at home.	I remained home.	Preposition Deletion
For the end to catch the pass was easy.	To catch the pass was easy for the end.	Subject Inversion
	The pass was easy for the end to catch.	Subject + Infinitive Inversion
	It was easy for the end to catch the pass.	Expletive 2

Paraphrase transformations, like nonparaphrase transformations, can add elements (*there*), delete elements (*at*), and change the relative positions of elements (*adverbs*); and a single transformation can do more than one of these things. But with this set of transformations, the sentence before and the sentence after the transformation means basically the same thing. Transformational grammar states that *John recovered the stolen goods* is related to *The stolen goods were recovered by John* by saying that the second is derived from the first by means of the passive transformation. The deep-structure grammar of a sentence is the grammar of the kernel sentence. In our example, *John* is the subject, and *goods* is the direct object in the deep structure of both the active and passive sentences. Any grammatical relationships (including incongruencies such as *inhaled chairs*) that exist in the kernel sentence before transformations are applied are retained in the derived sentences after transformations are applied. This, plus the fact that the paraphrase transformations do not happen to carry any meaning change, allows us to predict that these paraphrase transformations can be applied freely without changing the meaning.

Even those transformations which change or delete meanings are important. Consider, for example, sentences that are in some way deviant. This deviation from grammaticality is often used for special literary effects or for humor. Personification achieves its special effect because there is an incongruence between a nonanimate subject and a verb that requires an animate subject. Understanding the nature of the deviation and the fact that it remains no matter what transformations are applied helps a reader understand the deviations, and helps a writer use them effectively. Many modern poets use this kind of deviation, or semi-grammaticalness. Students who understand these deviations are more likely to recognize them when they occur accidentally in their own work. Moreover, students who understand the wide range of paraphrase transformations and the ways of conjoining and embedding sentences will be more apt to develop a sophisticated writing style. A preliminary study with ninth and tenth graders described in the May 1965 *English Journal* gives hope that this is true.

In conclusion, of the three grammars that have been considered in this article, only the transformational grammar handles in a complete manner discontinuous elements (*Mary tried the bikini on* as compared with *Mary tried on the bikini*); inversions (*The left fielder confidently caught the ball* as compared with *The left fielder caught the ball confidently*); deletions (*I saw the horse that is outside* as compared with *I saw the horse outside*); "co-occurrence" restrictions (*John didn't drink the carpet* as compared with *John didn't drink the milk*), dual functioning of a single item (for example, in the sentence *Someone used the inhaled chairs all morning,* the word *chairs* is the deep-structure direct object not only of the verb *used,* but also of the modifier *inhaled*); and relationships between structures (*Several boys were eating apples* as compared with *There were several boys eating apples*). Furthermore, of these three grammars, only the generative-transformational grammar generates rather than merely analyzes sentences.

In contrasting these three grammars, one last point should be made. Structural grammarians have greatly criticized traditional grammarians for having a grammar designed primarily to change or control language skills. The structural model therefore developed as a descriptive grammar rather than a prescriptive grammar, and structuralists very seldom made statements about what *should* be said, but were content rather to record what *was* said. Structural grammar, which merely describes either speech or writing, is therefore a grammar of performance. As far as the diagrams are concerned, traditional grammar also is primarily concerned with performance, but it differs from structural grammar, in that it treats mostly written, rather than spoken, performance. In the nonformal traditional grammar, normative statements were made relating to what *should* be said or written. But since the normative statements of traditional grammar did not have any formal structure, they were random and incomplete. Now that we have a grammar which is able to deal with larger aspects of language, and which has the formal machinery to make accurate yet nontrivial generalizations, we have a grammatical model which has more potential as a teaching tool than either traditional or structural grammars could possibly have. This added power is being used effectively in some experimental classes, and many major textbook publishers have either prepared, or are in the process of preparing, transformational textbooks. They range in level from the primary grades through advanced college courses.

There is no indication, however, that transformational grammar will immediately supersede all other models. Although traditional grammar, which was imported from England in the 1700's, had its strongest influence before World War II, its philosophy is still a major influence today. Likewise there are many structural linguists who are making important contributions today, although the period of their greatest influence was in the 1930's, 1940's, and early 1950's. At the present time among scholars, the transformational model is the most highly respected, but it holds its place only precariously, with some grammarians clinging to the old while others are searching for new and even better models.

BIBLIOGRAPHY

Clark, Stephen W. *Analysis of the English Language,* 1851. One of the first attempts to use diagrams essentially the same as those in common use by traditionalists today.

Dykema, Karl W. "Where Our Grammar Came From," *College English,* 22 (April 1961), 455–465. This article shows that many aspects of present traditional grammar have their origins in classical Greek and Latin grammars.

Fries, Charles Carpenter. *The Structure of English: An Introduction to the Construction of English Sentences.* New York: Harcourt, Brace & World, 1952. The first thorough treatment of English syntax with the structural model. Adaptations of the analysis procedure outlined in this book are frequently employed by structuralists.

Gleason, Henry A., Jr. *Introduction to Descriptive Linguistics*, Second Edition. New York: Holt, Rinehart and Winston, 1961. This book is very popular as a text for introductory linguistics classes. It contains an excellent bibliography of the structural-descriptive linguistics approach.

——. *Linguistics and English Grammar*. New York: Holt, Rinehart and Winston, 1965. Part One, "Historical Background" (pp. 3–86), contains a very thorough and penetrating discussion of the history of grammars in America.

Hartung, Charles V. "The Persistence of Tradition in Grammar," *Quarterly Journal of Speech*, 48 (April 1962), 174–186. In this article Mr. Hartung defends the thesis that grammarians tend to be conservative. Many ties between classical Greek and Latin grammars and present traditional grammar are shown.

Hogan, Robert F., ed. *The English Language in the School Program*. Champaign, Illinois: NCTE, 1966. This anthology of structural and transformational articles is especially useful to the English teacher. It contains an annotated bibliography of generative-transformational materials.

House, Homer C., and Harman, Susan Emolyn. *Descriptive English Grammar*, Second Edition. Englewood Cliffs, New Jersey: Prentice-Hall, Inc. 1950. Despite the word *descriptive* in the title, this is a typical traditional textbook, and one that has widespread use in English grammar classes at the college level. It contains a good bibliography of traditional and early structural-descriptive books.

Nilsen, Don L. F. "New Diagrams for Old," *The English Record*, 16, 1 (October 1965), 20–23, 34–36. This article attempts to show some of the ways that the traditional diagrams are inadequate and, further, that transformational diagrams are not inadequate in the same ways.

——. "Relationships Between Traditional and Transformational Grammars," *The English Leaflet*, 65, 2 (1966), 4–12. This article attempts to show how transformational grammar has stronger roots in traditional grammar than it does in structural grammar.

——. "Transformation and Development of Style," *The English Record*, 17, 2 (December 1966), 38–43. It was in this article that the author first proposed the distinction between paraphrase and nonparaphrase transformations.

Reed, Alonzo, and Kellogg, Brainerd. *Higher Lessons in English: A Work on English Grammar and Composition* . . . , 1877. A revision of the Clark diagrams to the point that they are hardly distinguishable from the diagrams used in present traditional texts.

Thomas, Owen. "Grammatici Certant," *The English Journal*, 52, 5 (May 1963), 322–326. A clear and illuminating historical survey of grammars in America.

Zidonis, Frank. "Generative Grammar: A Report on Research," *The English Journal*, 54 (May 1965), 405–409. Frank Zidonis reports that in a two-year experiment with ninth and tenth graders, those who used the transformational model made significantly fewer errors, and at the same time wrote sentences of "greater structural complexity" than did those who used nontransformational grammar.

NOTES ON THE CONTRIBUTORS

Mario Pei is a linguist, teacher, and author of numerous books and articles on language. Perhaps his most famous works are *The Story of Language* and *The Story of English*. Most recently he has edited a *Glossary of Linguistic Terminology* (1966) and a communications guide to the vocabularies of twenty different fields, *Language of the Specialists* (1966). Professor Pei's fame as an accomplished polyglot is almost legendary. He has lectured, for example, in French, Italian, German, Dutch, Czech, and Romanian, and his speaking knowledge extends well beyond these. He has been a lecturer for the Foreign Policy Association, the Modern Language Association, The Voice of America, Radio Free Europe, and various professional groups. During World War II he was active in the preparation of linguistic projects to aid the war effort.

Born in Rome, Italy, Mario Pei came to the United States in 1908 and was educated in New York parochial schools. He was graduated from City College in 1925, and received his Doctor of Philosophy degree from Columbia University in 1932. He has been Professor of Romance Philology at Columbia since 1952.

William F. Marquardt is the Coordinator of Programs in Teaching English as a Second Language, School of Education, New York University. He is the author of many scholarly articles and papers. A native of Wisconsin, he received his B.A. and M.A. degrees from the University of Wisconsin and his Ph.D. from Northwestern University.

Katharine Le Mée currently teaches French at Columbia College. She received her B.A. and M.A. degrees from the University of Rochester and has done post-graduate work in kinesics under the direction of D. Lincoln Canfield. She is now working toward her doctorate in Romance Philology at Columbia University.

Don L. F. Nilsen is Coordinator of the Teacher Education Program at the University of Michigan's English Language Institute. With his wife, who is also a linguist, he is co-author of *Pronunciation Contrasts in English* (1967) and is a frequent contributor to scholarly journals. He received his B.A. degree from Brigham Young University and his M.A. degree from American University. He is currently preparing for his Ph.D. degree in linguistics at the University of Michigan.